THE MONEY PIRATES

SECOND EDITION

*Best Book on America's Money and
Unfair Taxation Ever Published!*

Lieutenant Colonel William A. Howle, AUS, Ret.

KENDALL/HUNT PUBLISHING COMPANY
4050 Westmark Drive   Dubuque, Iowa 52002

Printed in the United States of America
10 9 8 7 6 5 4 3 2 1

INFORMATION FOR READERS

This is the second edition of THE MONEY PIRATES. Corrections, deletions and additions have been made.

Special thanks to Anne Cronin and John Tiffany of Liberty Library for editorial suggestions and help.

Manuscript preparation by Cathy and Anthony Tao.

Illustrations vary in size to fit the space available.

Permission is granted to reproduce a single chapter or parable provided the author is given credit. More than that requires permission from the author. Cartoons or written material copyrighted by other authors require permission from that author.

Credit for sources is given in the text instead of with footnotes. Where no credit for a source is given, that quote is commonly known or is from "Famous Quotations On Money" available from America's Promise Ministries, PO Box 157, Sandpoint, Idaho 83864. Also available from the same publisher is the popular cartoon-style illustrated "BILLIONS FOR THE BANKERS; DEBTS FOR THE PEOPLE," by Sheldon Emery.

Let us vote for the United States envisioned by Franklin, Jefferson and Lincoln-- economic prosperity based on the medium of exchange that will do the job, **unborrowed currency** issued by our United States Treasury instead of **borrowing** the currency issued by our central bank.

Lieutenant Colonel William A. Howle, AUS, Ret.

CONTENTS

PREFACE

Government spends the **wrong kind** of money. It should spend **unborrowed** money instead of **borrowed** money.

THE THIRTEENTH BANK

The potential power of this bank seal is awesome. This bank seal, if used by Uncle Sam, would change the Federal Government from trillions of dollars in debt to a debt-free government!

There are 12 Federal Reserve Banks owned and operated by bankers. Let's request Congress to establish a 13th owned and operated by the United States Treasury. Its name would be, "U. S. Treasury Bank of Washington, D. C." The Federal Reserve Notes issued by THE THIRTEENTH BANK, "our" bank, would be identical in appearance to the notes issued by the twelve Federal Reserve Banks, "their" banks, except for the seal.

As soon as Congress establishes THE THIRTEENTH BANK, Uncle Sam will get from it all the money he needs. It will be unborrowed, debt-free money to the Federal Government and **tax saving**, interest-free money to us citizens.

The need for us to pay interest on government debt with our taxes will disappear, the government will have no debt.

When Uncle Sam gets money from the THIRTEENTH BANK, it will be UNBORROWED MONEY, the only kind government should spend.

Never again will government borrow money.

A MONEY PIRATE IN GUMBOLAND

"Do you know what a bond is?"

"Certainly, a bond means debt. Buying things with bonds doubles and triples the original price."

Whiz's answer surprised Box. Here he was in the jungle talking to a witch doctor who was wiser than the 535 leaders of the United States...

The events leading up to this conversation were these:

In 1913, America's biggest bankers said to Congress, "We want to add a hidden interest charge on the medium of exchange of the United States."

Congress said, "How can you do that?"

The bankers said, "With bonds. Appoint us the central bank of the United States. We will issue bank notes. You will order the U. S. Treasury to issue bonds and give them to us for our bank notes. You order Treasury to print our notes for us, label them United States dollars and use them as the nation's currency. The people will be fooled into thinking the Treasury is creating money instead of IOU's. Interest on government bonds is a hidden interest charge on the people's currency which they pay with their taxes."

"No deal," said Congressman Charles Lindbergh, "the U. S. Constitution empowers Congress to create and spend unborrowed dollars into the economy."

But the majority of Congress said, "This scam will make you bankers rich but how will it benefit us congressmen and senators? And will the people catch on?"

The bankers said, "We, plus the corporate managers we finance, will reward you with all kinds of political payoffs and provide all the money you need to get reelected. As for the people, polls show they want more money for themselves but never give a thought as to how their currency is created."

This satisfied Congress which enacted the Federal Reserve Act of 1913 permanently enslaving in debt the citizens of the United States.

As the original central bankers died they were replaced with others. In 1991, one of them, J. Martindale Exeter Box, flying to South Africa, fell asleep. He was rudely awakened. "We found out you are a central banker," explained the passengers as they shoved him out of the airplane's door. They understood what central bankers do to people.

Box fell 40,000 feet landing in a soft spot in the garden of Chief Gumbo's palace. After introductions, Gumbo invited Box to lunch. "Lucky break for me," said Gumbo, "I watch the wars on TV and the democracies have the best airplanes, tanks and bombs so I want democracy for Gumboland. All we have is spears cut from trees. As a central banker, you are admired as a leader in spreading democracy to all nations."

Box said, "I've never heard a central banker described in just that way before."

Gumbo said, "Don't be modest. I want you to tell me how to convert to democracy and order tanks, guns and bombs. You can do that for me, can't you?"

"Well, uh, yes," said Box. "I can fix you up with democracy, free enterprise, free trade, foreign involvement, foreign aid, capitalism, a mountain of unpayable debt and Democrats or Republicans. Actually, both will do anything to get elected so you had just as well have a one party system."

A man with a necklace of bones came in. Gumbo said, "This is Whiz, our medicine man and witch doctor. In his spare time, between spells and incantations, he is my treasurer. Please explain democracy to him and how to get guns into the hands of everybody."

Box couldn't believe his good luck. He, a central banker, was being invited to loot another country. Box said, "Glad to meet you, Whiz. Gumboland is in debt how much?"

Whiz said, "Gumboland uses the logical money system advocated by Thomas Jefferson so we have no debt. Our currency is treasury notes. The amount of taxes our citizens are willing to pay next year, Chief Gumbo spends into the economy this year. Outgo is balanced by income. When necessary, Chief Gumbo controls the amount of money in circulation by spending more or less."

Crisis! All Central Bankers swear to murder their own mothers before any nation is allowed to use a logical money system. It matters not if the system is named a Tom Jefferson System, Tallies System, New York Colony System, Guernsey Treasury-Note System or Honest Abe Lincoln System, no nation (Except Guernsey.) is to be allowed to use it. If one major nation used a logical system, other nations would be sure to follow. Box thought fast. He must convince Whiz to change to a borrowed bank-note system. Otherwise, it would be necessary to order the president of the United States to send in the marines and destroy Gumboland for its own good. Modern civilized governments must be kept free from logic.

Box said, "Whiz, Chief Gumbo wants a democracy. Now I ask you, what nation has the most debt?"

"The United States."

"Correct, and there's your answer. The more debt you have, the more democracy you have. Let me quote you the timeless words of Alexander Hamilton, first Secretary of the Treasury and the man who led the United States into endless debt. (This quote from MONEY CREATORS by Gertrude Coogan, page 192.) 'A national debt, if it is not excessive, will be a national blessing; a powerful cement of union; a necessity for keeping up taxation and a spur to industry.' Understand?"

"Sounds like a man trying to start a central bank."

Box said, "You hit the nail on the head. That's exactly what happened. Hamilton bribed congressmen with inside information and fathered the United States' first central bank. The ungrateful people killed it and the second one, but the third one, named the Federal Reserve System, is thriving. It is so successful that in just the past year it has piled up the biggest debt in history!"

Whiz said, "Debt is good?"

"Yes, yes, as Hamilton said, it is a national blessing. Do you know what a bond is?"

"Certainly, a bond means debt. Paying for things with bonds doubles and triples the original price."

This answer almost floored Box. Here he was in the jungle talking to a witch doctor who was wiser than the 535 leaders of the United States. Unless Whiz could be convinced that government debt was desirable and would accept the scam of "government bonds for bank notes," Box knew he had a lost cause. A central banker never passes up a chance to steal money legally so, in hopes it would convince Whiz, he decided to demonstrate how the scam works and explain its advantages to those in control of a government including the personal rewards for Gumbo and Whiz.

Box said, "We need a stack of blank paper, an engraver and a printing press."

Whiz called in Elstinko, "El" for short, an outdoor plumber who did a little engraving on the side.

Box said, "El, engrave some central bank-note currency and some Gumboland government bonds. The bonds will pay 6%, uh, make that 10%. 10% interest will build up Gumboland's national debt faster."

The next day the engraving was finished and Box printed ten million dollars in currency and instructed Whiz to print ten million dollars in bonds. Box put the money in one stack and told Whiz to put the bonds in a second stack. Then Box took a good look at the engravings on top of the two stacks.

4

The stack of ten million dollars in **GUMBOLAND BONDS** contained bonds of many denominations all the way from one hundred dollars to a million. Here is the one on top:

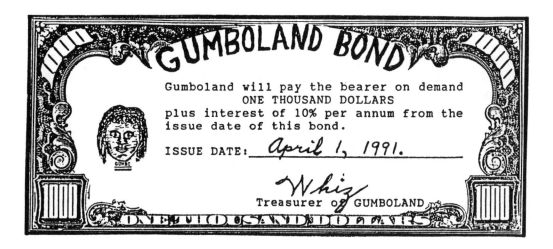

The stack of ten million dollars in bank-note currency contained notes of many denominations all the way from one dollar to one thousand. Here is the $5.00 bill on top:

Box said, "These engravings are not very artistic. You did say that El is an engraver, didn't you?"

Whiz said, "El is an amateur engraver. The only tool he has is a 10¢ ball point pen. He is a professional outdoor plumbing specialist and for that he has the best shovel money can buy."

Box said, "Well, let's go with what we've got. As your central banker the bank-note money is mine and as treasurer of Gumboland the government bonds are yours. Now, take a close look at this five dollar bill. See, in large letters it says 'GUMBOLAND CURRENCY,' and in small letters 'Federal Reserve Note.' I'm calling my central bank, 'Federal Reserve,' same as in the USA."

Whiz said, "It's plain to see that the money you have printed is genuine bank-note currency. The title plainly states, 'FEDERAL RESERVE NOTE' and there is a 'Federal Reserve Bank of Gumbo' bank seal printed on each note."

There was a slight pause. Box feared Whiz might know that bank-note currency is the money of a plutocracy. If so, that might kill the scam because Chief Gumbo had specifically requested that a democracy be established.

Whiz said nothing so Box continued, "Whiz, Chief Gumbo wants modern armament of all kinds. That takes tons of money. As your central banker I will provide you with all the money you want by buying your bonds. Any time you want more money, you print more bonds. A central bank's money is limitless, I can always create more for just the cost of printing. Well, Whiz, it's time for your first sale. Here is my ten million dollars in bank notes, give me your ten million dollars in bonds."

They exchanged the stacks of paper. Box now had the pieces of paper named bonds and Whiz had the pieces of paper named money. Box said, "With this exchange you have borrowed ten million dollars from my central bank. A year from now Gumboland will owe my bank $10,000,000.00 plus $1,000,000.00 in interest for a total of $11,000,000.00."

Whiz hesitated, "I don't see the advantage to Gumboland of this paper exchange."

Box said, "The advantage is to the leaders, you and Chief Gumbo. This money system will provide you with unlimited money to spend, create a rich investor class who will support you with their money and it will keep the common people on their knees under a burden of eternal debt."

Whiz said, "I love the people. It might be better to reprint this paper so that the bonds would be banker bonds and the money would be treasury notes."

Box said, "No, no, no. That would make the bankers pay the government for the privilege of banking. That's not what we want, we want the government paying the bankers."

Whiz said, "I still have my doubts."

Box said, "Another advantage of government bonds for bank notes is that after installing the system it will no longer be possible for Gumboland to have a balanced budget. This is advantageous for government leaders because they can pose as fighters for the people. They can rail against government waste, claim they are fighting against the special interests and promise to balance the budget next year. The people, not understanding money creation, will go for this charade and elect the same flim-flammers over and over again."

Whiz said, "I admit the people are ignorant on creation of a nation's currency but this bankers' scam worries me. I see it as growing debt for Gumboland's government with citizens paying more and more interest forever."

Box said, "Whiz, you've got it! Government debt always means interest charges for the people to pay with their taxes and that's the key to efficient government. I quoted Alexander Hamilton a moment ago. You may have missed this. He said debt is good because it is 'a necessity for keeping up taxation.' Think on that. You can keep your citizens in line with taxes. If they don't pay their taxes, throw them in jail. Tax them enough and they will eat out of your hand and lick your boots for just a promise of relief. In the USA, congressmen and senators adore the system and spend half their time thinking up new taxes and new ways to squeeze the people with a greater tax load."

Whiz said, "Well, I'll tell the chief what you said."

"Very good. Be sure to quote Alexander Hamilton saying that government debt is a national blessing. Then tell him that I calculate that eleven million dollars is about all the blessing you can handle the first year, but fortunately our Federal Reserve System has an escalation feature. Automatically your debt will be greater every year the rest of your life. Interest charges will rise, taxes will increase, prices will escalate and a dollar worth a dollar today will be worth about a penny thirty years from now."

Whiz started to leave but Box stopped him, "Be sure you tell Chief Gumbo that the USA uses our scam money system which proves it is the best and don't forget to tell him that we bankers know how to show our gratitude."

Satisfied that he had done a super sales job, Box celebrated in the local night spots.

The next morning, Box was awakened by two warriors with spears and escorted to Chief Gumbo's conference room. Gumbo and Whiz were there. Chief Gumbo said, "Box, we know a con man when we see one. We want no more of your bull that debt is good. However, you praised debt so much I have decided to be the central banker with you as the victimized citizen."

Box turned pale but managed to say, "No, I can't agree with that."

A warrior nudged Box in the ribs with the point of a spear.

"On second thought, I can agree with that."

Whiz said, "Last night we transferred your signature from a bank note to a bond we designed. Then we burned all the notes and bonds printed yesterday. Here, have a look at your bond."

Box read the bond and almost fainted. It stated he would pay Gumboland $1,000,000.00 at 10% interest. Here it is:

J . M. E . BOX BANK BOND

ONE MILLION DOLLARS

J. Martindale Exeter Box will pay Gumboland
$1,000,000.00
plus 10% interest per annum from the issue
date of this bond, April 1, 1991.

J.M.E. Box
Central Banker

Whiz said, "Would you like to sell your bond?"

Box looked at a spear under his nose and with great reluctance said, "Yes." Whiz handed a million dollars in Gumboland treasury notes to Box and Box handed Whiz the bond.

Whiz said, "Box, you have now borrowed $1,000,000.00 at 10% interest from Gumboland. At the end of the year you will owe us $1,100,000.00."

Box, in shock, was barely able to grasp the piece of paper Chief Gumbo handed him. Gumbo said, "This is your receipt for the office space you bought from me. It came to exactly one million dollars."

"Didn't know I bought any," mumbled Box as the meanest looking warrior took the million dollars from him.

"Wazzo is my IRS," chuckled Gumbo.

Box said, "I really don't need an office. I have a strong urge to return to the USA where the bankers and the politicians are in partnership."

Gumbo said, "Not yet. I have your bond for a million dollars bearing interest at 10%. At the end of this year you will owe me $1,100,000.00. How do you propose to pay?"

"I'll put it in the mail the minute I get back to the United States."

"No deal. Central bankers are money pirates and I wouldn't trust one at ten feet. They steal money surreptitiously from unsuspecting citizens with their government bonds for bank notes scam. In addition, the scam makes a nation a beggar to its own central bank. Mr. Box, I am not stupid. Here in Gumboland, I am the master of the banks and they will never be permitted to govern the economy of Gumboland. I will allow the banks to loan money but never will I permit them to issue Gumboland currency."

Box was astonished that a tribal chief really understood money.

Gumbo was enjoying himself and he said, "Box, you do know that a treasury note dollar is always worth more than a bank note dollar, don't you?"

Box said, "Yes, interest charges discount the value of bank notes but not treasury notes. The public has been brainwashed to believe the reverse. The people foolishly believe that bank issued money is good and treasury issued money is bad 'printing press' stuff."

Gumbo said, "Because of the interest charges paid to borrow them, bank notes automatically cause inflation forcing prices and taxes to rise."

Box said, "That's true but politicians like inflation. The interest on past borrowings can be paid off with cheaper dollars."

Gumbo said, "It's impossible to balance a budget with borrowed money."

"Which is what Federal Reserve Notes are," said Box, laughing as he recalled all the politicians who get elected claiming they are going to balance the budget. None of them ever say this is impossible until the Federal Government replaces borrowed money with unborrowed money. A government's greatest power, except for waging war, is its ability to spend unborrowed money.

Watching Box laugh Gumbo wondered if all central bankers are sociopaths. Another spasm of laughter shook Box. "Cleverest thing we bankers have accomplished over the years," he said, "is convincing the American people that if the U. S. Treasury creates money it has got to be gold or silver but if we bankers create money it's okay for it to be paper."

Chief Gumbo shook his head more in sorrow than disgust and said, "Americans are misled and poorly educated. Here in Gumboland we tell our people the truth and encourage them to enjoy questioning and learning."

Box had not been lectured to before. He was accustomed to telling lies and flim-flamming sympathetic senators on TV and sending them campaign contributions through carefully selected channels.

Gumbo said, "I'll make you an offer you can't refuse. I will buy back your office space and that will satisfy the principal of your debt and I will discount the interest to 5% provided you pay me now. $50,000.00 please."

Box wired for the money. It arrived within the hour. Box paid Gumbo and asked permission to leave.

Gumbo said, "You are an heir of Alexander Hamilton who favored for the United States a central bank patterned after the privately owned Bank of England and a government by the wealthy--a plutocracy. His great opponent, Thomas Jefferson, fought for a democracy and would have won had he been able to get into the Constitution his amendment to prevent borrowing by the government. Hamilton won the battle from the grave. In 1913, a bribed Congress delivered the United States into the hands of a consortium of bankers. Today America is a plutocracy. It has the trappings of democracy but the actual power is exercised by the majority owners of your Federal Reserve Banks in alliance with your top politicians."

Box had no rebuttal. Money pirates are exposed as the unconscionable scam artists they are when faced by people who understand their "government bonds for bank notes" scam.

Gumbo said, "Federal Reserve Notes are 'drop out' currency. Instead of staying in America's economy, Federal Reserve Notes are continually dropping out of circulation to go pay interest on government IOU's."

Box brightened, "Yes, but we bankers have an agreement that Congress will sell more bonds and reborrow our Federal Reserve Notes again and again and pay more and more interest."

Gumbo said, "What America needs is a treasury created currency that won't 'drop out,' one that is issued unborrowed so that it stays in the market place and keeps on circulating among the buyers and sellers of goods and services creating employment and prosperity for all the people."

Box kept his mouth shut. He did not think it wise to tell Gumbo that the American Bankers Association in alliance with the U. S. Congress will not permit the American people to use dollars created by their own United States Treasury.

Gumbo said, "Your visit has brought home to me plutocracy and the arms business feed on each other. Spears cut from trees is a better deal than that. Here is your $50,000.00. I have no desire to rob you but I hope you now know how it feels. You may go now."

Box returned to the land where the citizens are brainwashed into believing the money pirates are good citizens instead of what they actually are, the biggest thieves the world has ever seen. With America's money and economy under their control, it is no surprise they can elect the congressmen and senators they need to stay in power.

This story has a sad ending. The money pirates declared in their newspapers and on their TV stations that Gumbo was a mortal enemy of the U. S. and ordered the president to send in the CIA to pay local enemies to eliminate Gumbo and Whiz. In the following chaos, the marines were sent in to feed the people and a Federal Reserve

System was established to milk the economy. Thus, another would-be democracy became a plutocracy controlled by the central bankers.

(SPECIAL NOTE: The 12 Federal Reserve Banks are best described as a private corporation furthering the interests of the commercial banks. The owners of the commercial banks--the banks the public deals with--control the Federal Reserve Banks and, in turn, the entire Federal Reserve money monopoly. Congressmen and senators constantly brag that the Fed is independent of the U. S. Government so the citizens have no control over it whatsoever. This frees the Fed to continue working its bank notes for government bonds scam.)

CURRENCY UNCLE SAM SHOULD NOT USE

Pictured here is the currency Uncle Sam should NOT use. By agreement between the owners of the Federal Reserve banks and Congress it is the only currency we see in circulation. It is readily identifiable by its title, "FEDERAL RESERVE NOTE," and its bank seal. The seal on this one tells us that it was created by the Federal Reserve Bank of Chicago, IL. For 2½¢ the U. S. Treasury printed it for the Chicago bank.

We pay interest on every Federal Reserve Note dollar in circulation. That's asinine. A medium of exchange should be neutral at birth, not a means of profit for bankers who elect politicians. Here are all 12 Federal Reserve Bank seals:

THE CAUSE OF UNCLE SAM'S MONEY WOES

Uncle Sam's money woes are caused by his printing and selling bonds. The **interest** charges gobble up more than half the personal income taxes we pay leaving less than half for the Federal Government to spend on America's needs. Pictured here is a $100.00 United States Bond:

Our Constitution authorizes Congress to both create and borrow money. Because Uncle Sam can create money, he has no need to ever borrow any. He should quit selling U. S. Bonds.

Thomas Edison said, "If people ever get to thinking of bonds and (dollar) bills at the same time, the game is up...Here is the point: If our nation can issue a dollar bond it can issue a dollar bill. The element that makes the bond good makes the bill good also. The difference between the bond and the bill is that the bond lets the money brokers collect twice the amount of the bond and an additional 20 per cent, whereas the currency pays nobody but those who contribute...in some useful way." (See the Ford-Edison Chapter.)

Edison's words were applied to U. S. Bonds of large denomination. The bond pictured above isn't quite that expensive to taxpayers. This Savings Bond sells for $50.00. If the owner holds it to maturity, he will recover his investment of $50.00 plus $50.00 from us taxpayers.

CURRENCY UNCLE SAM SHOULD USE

In Chapter 1, the currency issued by **THE THIRTEENTH BANK** would be treasury-note money because **THE THIRTEENTH BANK** would be owned by the U. S. Treasury. To leave "Federal Reserve Note" as the title would be misleading. Shown here is the proper title for Uncle Sam's Treasury-note money. **"UNITED STATES NOTE"** should be appealing to all Americans.

U. S. Treasury created **UNITED STATES NOTES** are Uncle Sam's own money which he can spend directly out of the Treasury, no borrowing involved. **UNITED STATES NOTES** are debt-free to Uncle Sam and **tax savers** for us citizens.

Both bank notes and treasury notes are dollar bills. They are backed the same, not by gold, but by the faith and credit of the American people. Uncle Sam can spend either into the economy. If Uncle Sam spends Federal Reserve note dollars he plunges himself into debt; if he spends United States note dollars he incurs no debt. If he spends Federal Reserve note dollars he drowns in interest charges; if he spends United States note dollars he has no interest to pay.

Uncle Sam must quit borrowing Federal Reserve Notes and pay out only unborrowed money. Then he can balance expenditures with income. A sound economy is based on a sound currency system. For a sound economy with lower taxes, **UNITED STATES NOTES** are the answer.

The day the U. S. Government stops selling pieces of paper named U. S. Bonds will be **"FREEDOM FROM GOVERNMENT DEBT DAY."** As soon as our Federal Government replaces Federal Reserve Notes with United States Notes it must pay off its debt putting a **stop to the interest charges.** It may sound unreal to those who have not studied the problem but Uncle Sam cannot balance outgo with income if any interest is added onto outgo.

One plan for paying off the debt is Dr. Edward E. Popp's, "The U. S. Government's Debt Can Be Paid Off!" There are other plans but the basic idea is the same. Recall U. S. Bonds and IOU's that have been given away; pay off those that have been bought by legitimate investors.

Abraham Lincoln called United States Notes America's "greatest blessing."

Alexander Hamilton, who originally guided us into using the wrong kind of currency, repented six years before Burr killed him. Hamilton said in effect, "Bank notes are no good. Don't use them. Issue Treasury notes for U. S. currency." (Page 205, MONEY CREATORS by Gertrude M. Coogan.)

In 1994, Congressman Henry Gonzalez of Texas agrees with Lincoln and Hamilton.

You may not see any United States Notes in circulation. Our Federal Government, controlled by special interests, hides them in a vault.

As soon as a person understands the "Government IOU's for bank notes" scam, this question follows, "Why doesn't Congress use United States Notes?" Consider the machine called "X."

You own "X," the world's most marvelous machine. X is a money making machine that produces only on your command.

You are eager to get rich. X is designed to be installed in the United Sates Treasury. You install it there and order it to produce money. To your surprise, the money produced by X goes out all over the USA and is shared by all the citizens!

You don't like this. How can you be a member of the super rich elite if the darn machine shares the wealth with Average Americans? Some scroungy pirates come to see you and offer you gifts for X. You take the gifts, hand over X and order it to produce for them.

Aggravation! You now find that all citizens must have some of X's production. You go to the pirates and ask for their help. They offer to **loan** you X's production. What a silly offer! X is your property and it is producing money for the pirates only because you ordered it to do so.

All you need do is take back X and reinstall it in the Treasury where it will produce UNITED STATES NOTES as the nation's currency. **No borrowing from pirates required.** No Government debt, no paying of interest by citizens. No need to ever again print a United States Bond. Then you stop and think. If you do that, the pirates will quit giving you your political payoffs, so you agree to their offer.

X produces money for the pirates but **not Constitutional money!** The money X produces for the pirates is counterfeit Constitutional currency which the pirates have named Federal Reserve Notes. You refuse to give up your political payoffs so you declare the pirates' fraudulent currency to be United States money. Now in 1993, America is in recession because of an economy based on its faulty money system which requires Uncle Sam to pay a quarter of a trillion dollars in interest every year-- and going up!

Why don't you change the money system to a Constitutional no-debt, no-interest charges currency system, quit printing bonds, and give the United States a firm foundation for a sound economy? People who ask that question don't understand politics. Through their issuance and control of America's currency the pirates are all very rich with lots of rich friends. They all pay you well with political payoffs, allow you to rub shoulders with them and furnish the money for your reelection.

X is the Constitutional provision, "Congress is empowered to coin (create) money." You are Congress. The pirates are the owners of New York City's biggest banks who control the Federal Reserve System.

The best explanation of how the money pirates continue to get away with their "money system" of exchanging their bank notes created out of nothing for United States Bonds that pay them interest and, at the same time gives them control of America's economy, may be these words, "The few who can understand the system will either be so interested in its profits, or so dependent on its favors, that there will be no opposition from that class, while on the other hand, the great body of the people mentally incapable of comprehending the tremendous advantage that capital derives from the system, will bear its burdens without complaint and perhaps without even suspecting that the system is inimical to their interests." (Rothschild Brothers of London.)

Birthplace of Money

People tend to think money comes to a government from an outside source, for example, from a gold mine or from a building called a bank. It's the other way round. Government is the source of the legality we call money. The womb of U. S. money is eleven words, "Congress shall have power to coin money and regulate its value."

GOLD AND SILVER

When Mother Nature created gold did she proclaim, "I have created the medium of exchange for mankind?"

This chapter has a superb technical discussion by Peter Cook followed by less formal remarks by your author.

Aware that your author is one of those people who advocate replacing Federal Reserve Notes with United States Notes, a thoughtful citizen wrote a letter to me the gist of which was this:

"You seem to gloss over the fact that the Constitution requires U. S. money to be gold and silver coin only--no greenbacks. (Abraham Lincoln's United States Notes were called greenbacks.) In economic theory it may be that United States Notes are preferable to gold and silver coins. Frankly, I do not know but I lean that way. But it is incontrovertibly the law at present that money is gold and silver coin only. So until the Constitution can be amended, greenbackers have a serious problem and one they must face up to."

I thanked him for his thoughtful letter and by way of reply sent him the following written by Peter Cook, M. Sc., Monetary Science Publishing, Box 86, Wickliffe, OH 44092:

"DOES ARTICLE 1, SECTION 10, OF THE UNITED STATES CONSTITUTION ESTABLISH THAT ONLY GOLD AND SILVER IS LEGAL TENDER MONEY IN THE UNITED STATES?

As with any other law or statute, every saint, judge, lawyer and thief likes to bend the law to his favor. The proponents of a gold standard or gold redeemable currency are no exception. Many cite Article 1, Section 10, Clause 1, as the authority defining gold and silver coin as the only true legal tender money in the United States. Perhaps they arrive at that conclusion without reading Clause 2, of Article 1, Section 10, which as we shall see has strong bearing on the question.

Madison in Federalist #44 tells us the following: "The right of coining money, which is here taken from the States...they ought not be at liberty to substitute a paper medium in the place of coin... No one of these mischiefs is less incident to a power in the States to emit paper money, than to coin gold and silver." Madison is saying: States having the authority to emit paper money may very quickly assume the coining of gold and silver. Madison continues: Had every State a right to (coin) regulate the value of its coin, there might be as many different currencies as States"... Therefor, "The power to make anything but gold and silver (bullion or foreign coin at that time) a tender in payment of debts is withdrawn from the States"...

Article 1, Section 10, Clause 1, reads as follows in reference to money: "No State shall...coin Money; emit Bills of Credit; make any Thing but gold and silver Coin a Tender in Payment of Debts"... That last phrase quoted appears to support the proponents' case only if removed from the context of the full statement which is clearly an instruction to the States prohibiting their issue of money in any form, and dictating the form in which they must pay their debts. There is no statement nor implication that gold and/or silver coins were or are to be legal tender. In fact, when Article 1, Section 10, was written (1787) there was no U. S. coin of any kind. There was no official U. S. Treasury and no U. S. mint. The writers of Article 1, Section 10, most probably had little idea of what was to be a half or double eagle. It was five years later that the establishment of a mint was enacted. The first United States silver coins were minted in 1794, the first gold half-eagles in 1795. However, there was already a variety of foreign coin in circulation in the United States at that time.

In order to further clarify: "make any Thing but gold and silver Coin a Tender in Payment of Debts," we must consider that part of Clause 2, which reads: "and the net Produce of all Duties and Imposts, laid by any State on Imports or Exports, shall be for the Use of the Treasury of the United States;"... When we realize that Article 1, Section 10, is giving specific instructions to the States, we can see that the States are instructed to Tender (offer) only gold and silver coin in Payment of State's Debts to the United States Treasury.

The authors of Article 1, Section 10, understood well that in that period there were hundreds of banks in the 13 States printing paper money, promising redeemability in gold or silver. They also were aware that States printed their own money under the Articles of Confederation, and that some of that money, though much depreciated was still in circulation. Therefore, under such circumstances the bank-printed and state-printed paper money would be of little use or value to the Federal Government, because no one would want a distant state or bank paper money which could not be locally redeemed for gold or silver.

Thereupon, the authors of Article 1, Section 10, in spelling out the duties of the States wrote: "make anything but gold or silver Coin (foreign at that time) a Tender (offer) in Payment of (States') Debts (to the U. S. Treasury);"...

From this historical information we can see that Article 1, Section 10, Clause 1 and 2, were not written with any intention of establishing a "form" of legal tender money in the United States. The authors of the Constitution had already spelled out instructions for the establishment of a sound legal tender tax-redeemable money system in Article 1, Section 8, Clause 5 and 1. In Clause 5 of the original document the word "Money" is capitalized, which in consideration of English usage at the time leaves no question that it is a noun undefined. The word "coin" is not capitalized which again leaves no question that it is a verb denoting action (make, print, authorize).

With such unmistakable instructions there is no question that Congress under the supreme sovereignty of the people, has the authority to determine in what modern and convenient form Public Credit Money should be provided--for financing the National Government and the Free enterprise Economy. And by the authority of Clause 1, of Article 1, Section 8, Congress has the taxing authority to maintain a monetary equilibrium and thus regulate the volume, value and purchasing power of the public's money.

Under the Federal Reserve Act of 1913, the control of the money volume and value is in the hands of frivolous money managers over which the public, Congress nor the President have any meaningful control."

This excellent analysis by Peter Cook shows us the Constitution does not require that our money be gold and silver coin nor does it prevent us from using unborrowed treasury-note dollar bills created by our own United States Treasury.

The Constitution of the United States, Article 1, Section 8 gives orders to the Federal Government's Congress; Section 10 gives orders to the 13 states.

This distinction is of the utmost importance. Section 8 empowers Congress to coin money and regulate its value. Please note well that the empowerment does not read, "Congress is empowered to coin gold and silver coins only." If that is what the authors of the Constitution wanted to say, this was the place to say it. "Coin" means "create" or "issue."

In Section 10, the thirteen states are told: States are not authorized to mint money or issue note money. The U. S. Treasury will not accept currency issued by states in the past. The Treasury will not accept bank notes of state banks. The only money Treasury will accept is foreign coins of gold or silver. In about seven years when we establish a U. S. Mint, Treasury will accept U. S. silver dollars containing a certain number of grains of fine silver and also gold coins if we can get our hands on some gold from somewhere, decide how much gold to put in them and think of a name for them.

The gist of another letter I received was this: "I have seen nothing to convince me that a dollar is something other than a certain amount of silver. If you could clarify this puzzling matter so that a person of average intelligence could understand that a dollar can be something else, you would be doing the patriot community a great service."

Congress has enacted several laws designating that silver dollars will contain so many grains of fine silver. So, if the United States Mint mints a silver dollar it will contain the amount of silver designated by Congress. (As we all know, currently we use non-silver, "sandwich" coins.)

Congress enacted a law May 31, 1878 that is still on the books which requires the U. S. Treasury to keep in circulation $323 million of United States Notes. (See chapter entitled "THE U. S. TREASURY HIDES UNITED STATES NOTES FROM U. S. CITIZENS.") The law states $323 million in Treasury-note dollars, i. e. United States Notes, will be in circulation at all times. In an earlier chapter a 1953 United States Note is pictured. Eisenhower and Kennedy issued some. Currently, our central bank dominated Government has printed the required millions in $100.00 bills and hidden them in a vault.

From the two paragraphs above we see that Congress has enacted laws that dollars are both silver coins and printed pieces of paper.

What does the Supreme Court think? In 1869, the Supreme Court decided that Abraham Lincoln's United States Notes, the "greenbacks," were unconstitutional. In 1872 it reversed itself. In 1884, the Court assumed the role of Pilate, got out a big bowl of water and washed its eighteen hands and solemnly stated, "Money is a political matter, not a judicial matter, we made an awful mistake wrestling around with it in '69 and '72. We hereby hand this hot potato back to Congress and we don't care what Congress decides as long as we get our pay checks on time." (Paraphrased from Dr. Popp's "The Great Cookie Jar" pages 15 and 16.)

Unless the Supreme Court makes further rulings, money is whatever Congress says it is. Unfortunately this includes Federal Reserve Notes, the currency whose womb is debt. In your author's opinion, Federal Reserve Notes are unconstitutional because Article 1, Section 8 does not empower Congress to delegate money creation to an agency that is not an integral part of the Federal Government. The 12 Federal Reserve Banks are privately owned.

Suppose the Supreme Court changes its mind again and rules the authors of the Constitution intended the meaning of "Congress has the power to coin money," to be "Congress is empowered to mint silver coins as the currency of the United States and nothing else shall be a legal tender. All debts public or private will be paid by silver coins passing from one hand to another. Further, all Federal Reserve Notes will be replaced by silver coins immediately. Further, since the national debt of $4 trillion is a paper dollar debt all United States Bonds will be paid off immediately with silver dollar coins."

The Secretary of the Treasury panicked and went to see the president. "I've got to mint 4,000,000,000,000 silver dollars and I must get my hands on sixty million tons of silver immediately."

The president said, "Well, borrow it. You know that we solve all our problems by borrowing money."

Germany and Japan said no. Back to the president went the secretary. "Nobody will loan us the money."

"We live on borrowed money. This is a **crisis.** What do we do?"

"Better call your boss," advised the secretary.

The president picked up his telephone and when his boss came on the line the president said to his boss, "Hello, Alan..."*

* The Chairman of the Federal Reserve Board.

FOUR LOGICAL MONEY SYSTEMS

KING HENRY AND THE TALLIES MONEY. Hop into my Time Machine. It is wintertime in not so merry Ye Olde England. The year is 1110. The king is Henry the First, fourth son of William the Conqueror and he's broke.

Despondent, the king walked from the royal suite at the top of his castle to the carpenter shop in the basement. Pete, the carpenter, was stacking boards. "Pete," said the King, "I'm broke. Got neither gold nor silver."

Pete said, "Beg pardon, sire, you are the richest man in all of England. Gold and silver are metals. They can be used for money but they are not money per se."

"What's with that per se? What does per se mean?"

"Per se is Latin for of itself. In plain English what I'm telling you, Henry--that is sire, sir--is that just because gold is a valuable metal, that doesn't necessarily make it money."

"Okay," said Henry, "tell me how I'm so rich."

"Use your taxing powers. Any citizen that doesn't pay his taxes, chop his head off. One example and zip, no more trouble collecting taxes."

"I agree with you, Pete, except there is almost no money out there in the hands of the people. England's king ahead of me sent most of England's money to Germany to buy soldiers to fight our last two wars. The fact is there is so little money in the hands of the people it's not worth the expense of collecting it."

"Henry, we are going to correct the shortage of money. I'll show you how. See this stack of little flat sticks of wood? Notice how I've marked and notched them? Now, I'm splitting them into halves. This stick is worth a pound (a couple of $$ for you folks that don't dig English.) this one two, and this one is worth a hundred! All together, I've created a 100,000 pounds!"

"Fiddlesticks," sniffed the king. "Looks like big sticks whittled into little sticks."

"Come now, sire," said the carpenter to the king. "All you need do is publish a royal edict that your sticks are money, that a year from now citizens must pay their taxes with them and in addition to the little sticks you have a bigger stick saved as a chopping block. The sticks are counterfeit proof because you spend only one half and keep the other half in your treasury until taxes are collected at which time the halves must match or tally. That's why this is Tallies-money. So, issue your edict and spend lots of Tallies so there will be plenty of money in the hands of the people. Tell your tax collector that next year he must collect in taxes the same amount of money you spend this year. In that way you will keep your budget balanced."

Light went on in the king's head. "I'll do it. England will have prosperity. Kneel, Sir Pete!" And the king whipped out his sword. "I dub thee Royal Economist."

Ol' Pete was already kneeling but hearing this, he moaned loudly falling prone before the king and kissing the king's feet effusively. "Not that," he cried in anguish. "Call me a silly idiot but don't ever call me an economist, PLEASE."

Said Henry, "I understand. I undub thee economist and dub thee the Royal Treasurer."

Here is a generalized sketch of a piece of Tally money:

England's Tallies Money System was a logical money system. No matter how much money King Henry spent his only costs were manufacturing and administration. Money spent and collected equalled so the king had a balanced budget. The king paid no interest so his money kept its value i.e. there was no inflation. It was counterfeit proof and it created no debt for the government nor interest charges for the people.

Logical money systems must follow this rule: What goes out must come back in. The amount of money spent or loaned out of a treasury must later be repaid by collection of taxes, loans and etc. The Tallies demonstrated this perfectly.

Tallies were cumbersome and the king didn't spend enough of them to meet England's need for currency. They should have been converted to treasury notes but sad to say they were not and this provided an argument for bank notes. However, the Tallies kept England debt-free for over 500 years and were partially used until 1826 when the last of them were burned in the furnace of the House of Parliament.

King Henry could have appointed a couple of dukes as his "Royal Bank" and directed them to create the tally-stick money. Then the king could have borrowed the money from the dukes and paid them interest. They, in turn, would give the king political payoffs. In other words, King Henry could have done the same insane thing the U. S. Federal Government did in 1913 and continues to this day.

Yes, King Henry could have appointed some dukes to create England's money. A dangerous thing to do! History shows that money creators soon become the masters of kings, presidents and legislative bodies. They control the world by enslaving all nations with loans of their bank-note currencies.

In the United States today the Federal Reserve creates and controls our money (except for coins). The Federal Reserve money system makes the rich richer and the poor poorer. This bewilders our money ignorant Congress which enacts all kinds of band-aid legislation but never considers correcting our flawed money system. "The Federal Reserve System is one of the most corrupt institutions the world has ever seen." So said Rep. Louis T. McFadden, Chairman of the U. S. Banking and Currency Commission for 22 years.

THE "BILLS" MONEY OF THE COLONY OF NEW YORK.

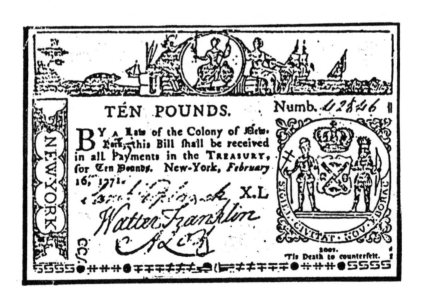

The pictured Ten Pound Bill issued by the Colony of New York in 1771 was sent to me by Dr. Edward E. Popp, the author of "The Great Cookie Jar" and "The U. S. Debt Can Be Paid Off." Jim Townsend published Dr. Popp's comments on this Bill in "The National Educator," Box 333, Fullerton CA 92632. Slightly edited here are Dr. Popp's comments:

"A government should not borrow the money it spends. It must spend money into the economy but every penny of it should be unborrowed. A prudent government body will use this procedure so it may operate without incurring debts.

"The government of England followed that procedure by issuing Tally sticks to serve as currency from 1100 A. D. to 1694 A. D. During those years England incurred no debt. The Colony of New York followed the same procedure for a number of years prior to 1776 by issuing Bills. These Bills paid for the colony's needed expenditures. A tax was levied on the public in an amount equal to the amount of the Bills paid out. The Government, in turn, received and redeemed these Bills when they were presented as payment for these taxes.

"From the time these Bills were paid out until the time they were used as payment for taxes, these Bills were used as currency by the people. Any item the government will receive as a payment due it, the people will use as currency among themselves.

"Any governmental body in the world can, by following the example of the Colony of New York, issue debt-free, interest-free currency and pay it into circulation for its needed expenditures. It then will be able to operate at all times without incurring debt and the people will have interest-free currency." That is the money/tax system the USA should be enjoying this very day.

Dr. Edward E. Popp, author of THE GREAT COOKIE JAR and many essays on money, a wonderful American and fighter for logical money died June 15, 1991. A great loss for the USA.

Dr. Popp's statement that any nation can use debt-free, interest-free currency, that is to say, use treasury notes instead of bank notes brings to mind the billions the USA gives away every year on foreign aid. If all the nations threw off the tyranny of the bankers and used a logical money system, our politicians would lose their excuse for throwing away our money overseas. In the meantime couldn't we put foreign aid on a voluntary basis?

We who think the bankers' monopoly of the world's money is a tragedy for the human race are appalled to see the nations of the world throwing off Communism only to throw themselves into the avaricious arms of the central bankers. They are exchanging one tyranny for another. The United States threw off the tyranny of the English bankers in 1781. Hopefully, we'll throw off the tyranny of their heirs, the owners of the Federal Reserve Banks, one of these days.

THOMAS JEFFERSON'S LOGICAL MONEY SYSTEM. "THE MAKING OF AMERICA, The Substance and Meaning of The Constitution" is a wonderful book written by W. Cleon Skousen. On page 498 we find that although Jefferson favored a metallic medium of exchange in peacetimes, he devised a logical paper money system for wartime that will operate perfectly in war or peace. In 1994, Jefferson's money system would be the greatest gift Congress could give America.

In reading Jefferson's words, we must remember Federal Reserve Notes never existed before 1913 and by "federal currency " he meant note money created by the U.S. Treasury. He certainly did not mean bank notes, he abhorred bank notes and, in fact, warned us that bank notes used as our currency would steal our property from us. A modern version of Jefferson's federal currency is the UNITED STATES NOTE pictured in an earlier chapter of this work. Here is Skousen describing Jefferson's logical money system:

"Jefferson...conceived of an ingenious device by which the American people could borrow from themselves without paying any interest. The following quotations from his writings will emphasize three points.

1. In a time of crisis, issue whatever federal currency is necessary to save the nation.
2. At the same time impose a tax of a comparable amount to redeem the extra currency within a designated time.
3. By this means the money goes out to buy the goods and services needed for the war and then is siphoned back into the treasury through taxes after it has done its work, thereby avoiding any long-range inflation."

Jefferson's Rule is, "What the government spends, it must tax back in." How simple, how sensible! Now comes the reminder that the money spent by the government must be its own unborrowed treasury notes. Government cannot pay interest and follow the "Jefferson Rule." The instant that the bookkeeping add-on of interest is added to the money spent by government, the government is out of balance and presenting the sorry spectacle our 535 people who govern America present every year when they write the budget for the coming year and tell all those lies they are going to reduce the deficit. It's difficult to believe that we have 535 people running the country and only Henry Gonzalez can add 2 + 2 and get 4.

THE ENGLISH CHANNEL ISLAND OF GUERNSEY was impoverished, an economic basket case, 176 years ago. It had debts and was being washed away by the sea. It did have some people who could think logically, the opposite of a committee of our Congress. One of them said, "Our government is cutting our throats by borrowing the bank-note money of the Bank of England (England's Federal Reserve System). Instead, let's have our own treasury create our own currency."

Beginning in 1816, they did just that and today Guernsey has 60,000 residents enjoying a high standard of living, NO UNEMPLOYMENT, a modern infrastructure and NO government debt. Here are two Guernsey treasury notes:

These Guernsey Treasury notes, being free of debt and interest charges, work like magic. Here is a report from Ken Bohnsack, chairman of Sovereignty: "Guernsey took itself from a huge debt, unemployment and crumbling infrastructure in 1816 by issuing money, (spending it into the economy for Guernsey's needs and) taxing it back in the form of small butcher and import taxes. (Taxes can be small when there is no interest to pay on government debt.)

"Guernsey built capital projects, which is building wealth into your country. With that goes the production of steel, cement and heavy equipment with an increase in employment.

"Guernsey has continued to do this and never has inflation. They have rid themselves of all their debts. Prior to this they had debts so great they were paying 80% of their total income in interest alone. That's what we are heading for in the

USA. It is estimated that by the year 2000 interest on the federal debt will have reached a trillion dollars."

"..that by the year 2000 (six years from now) interest on the federal debt will have reached a trillion dollars!" Congress will raise our taxes to pay it, of course, and do nothing to save us from the Federal Reserve bankers. In fact, most of our top leaders are members of David Rockefeller's organization of top bankers and top world leaders. They meet each year and plan how to run the world on the taxes the American people pay. Their meetings are private and as they own the mainstream media the meetings of the Bilderbergers and Trilateralists are rarely mentioned.

They aim to merge the USA into a world government. Americans are nothing special to them except as cash cows, builders of arms, world policemen and mercenary soldiers. They are **"one-worlders" and "free traders."**

We who want to keep our USA as our nation and not be governed by the UN think Americans are special people deserving a government that will protect their interests. American workers should be protected by a 10% duty on **all** goods coming into the United States. Such a tariff would not stop foreign trade, all foreign goods able to compete with the 10% tariff added on would continue to be imported.

The touted global economy is great for nabobs and wealthy investors but it is the United States economy that is vital to workers.

United States Notes would give us the same prosperity Guernsey enjoys. Please read "The Guernsey Experiment." This 36 page booklet is proof that any nation desiring prosperity can have it. It is available from sources listed under references.

One wonders if there is a single congressman in Washington who is familiar with the prosperity of Guernsey. On the other hand, the secret thinking in Washington may be that it's best to keep the people under control with a burden of debt and overtaxation.

TWO MONEY SYSTEMS SPAWNED BY GREED

Hop in the Time Machine, fasten your seat belt, we are going to Amsterdam this time. The calendar is blurred but the date is about 1592, America having been discovered a hundred years before. We are going to meet the fellow in the picture on the left, Otto Katzenjammer. He's a goldsmith making jewelry from gold and silver. He has the reputation of being the most successful goldsmith who ever lived. This artist's rendition of him is enshrined in England's Salisbury Cathedral.

In Amsterdam, we saw a big sign on a building, OTTO KATZENJAMMER, GOLDSMITH. I spoke to the pretty Dutch girl behind the counter, "Herr Katzenjammer, please."

"He's not here," she said, "he's next door in his loan office."

"We thought we would find him busy making bracelets, rings and things."

"He is the owner but he hasn't made jewelry himself for many years. He stays busy making loans."

Next door we introduced ourselves. "Just call me O.K. Everybody calls me that," said Herr Katzenjammer.

"We thought you would be goldsmithing."

"Merchants bring gold to me for safekeeping and I got into the loan business when I discovered I could write more than one receipt for the same gold. Excuse me, here comes Herr Schmitz to borrow 1,000 guilders. Hi, Herr Schmitz, how do you want the money?"

"Ten 100's will be fine," said Schmitz.

Schmitz signed a promissory note for the 1,000 guilders at 6% interest and O. K. took from a drawer a very thick pad of engraved documents. Each document proclaimed, "THIS IS A RECEIPT FOR 100 GOLD GUILDERS payable on demand from OTTO KATZENJAMMER, GOLDSMITH. O. K. scrawled his initials on ten of them and handed them to Herr Schmitz.

Schmitz departed and O. K. said, "Except for change, my gold receipts are the money of Amsterdam. Gold coins are heavy and a bother to use. Everybody prefers paper."

I said, "Your receipts are for gold. Where's the gold?"

"Everybody says my receipts are good as gold so I don't need any gold. Everybody uses my receipts, they'll buy anything in Amsterdam. I do keep a small supply of guilders on hand in case somebody insists that I cash one of my receipts. Hey, Hans, come over please and take over the loan desk."

Hans sat down behind the loan desk and O. K. took us across the street for lunch. He informed us that he had taught Hans to write OK as illegibly as he did so nobody could tell the difference. He could leave at any time and Hans would loan the gold receipts. O. K. paid for our lunch with one of his five guilder gold receipts. For change he received several small gold coins that were quarter guilders.

I should have kept my mouth shut but I couldn't help blurting out, "Neat, you initial a little piece of paper and get real gold in change!"

"You ain't seen nuthin' yet," said O. K. "Half of Amsterdam was built with my gold receipts. Let's get into the carriage at the curb." We climbed into the carriage and toured the city. Parks, buildings, public works, businesses and housing had all been built with O. K's gold receipts. Passing a huge block of apartments, O. K. said, "I financed these."

"Who owns them?" I asked.

"I do now. Builder couldn't meet his payments, I had to foreclose."

We rounded a bend and vivid colors overwhelmed us. "Best and biggest tulip farm in the whole world. It was unfortunate but I had to foreclose on the original owner," O. K. said.

We came to a large, beautiful park. Said O. K., "I gave this park to the city. Tremendous good will came of it."

We came to the docks. There was a large business park and many ships all labeled, "Katzenjammer Shipping."

"Foreclosure?"

"Yes, original owner couldn't pay the interest charges."

"How much of Amsterdam do you won?"

"Adding the holdings of my silent partners to mine we own about a third of the city."

"Who are your silent partners?"

O. K. said, "That, sir, is an impertinent question. How can several well-placed local politicians remain silent partners if I give out their names?"

"You're right, we do it the same way in America."

"Better get back to the office," said O. K.

Back at the office, O. K. pointed out his strongroom. "Safest and best strongroom in the whole world. Years ago, when I first got into the loan business, I would have as much as a million guilders in there. That was before I learned that I could write receipts for gold without having any. Just think, most of the building of Amsterdam was paid for with receipts for gold that never existed."

A customer came in to pay off his loan. He placed 2,000 guilders in gold receipts on the counter. "That pays the principal," he said, "and here's the interest." He placed 120 gold guilder coins on the counter. "My promissory note, please."

O. K. handed the customer his promissory note and he left. O. K. put the gold coins in his cash drawer and dropped the gold receipts into a large stove. "The stove is my incinerator."

He continued, "See how neat this entire operation is? I create money when I initial my gold receipts but I do so only when I receive a promissory note for that amount plus interest. Later, when my customer pays off his loan I insist he pay the interest in gold coin. As you just saw, I return his promissory note, keep the gold coins and drop the receipts into the incinerator. I create and extinguish money--at a profit."

"Who fires the incinerator?"

O. K. got this strange look on his face and stuttered, "W-well..., I do. Every evening." Pause. "I'm in trouble. About two years ago I realized I didn't need to burn up all that good money so I substituted waste paper for it. In no time I was richer than King Midas and took up gambling, horse racing, wild women and junk bonds. At the same time, a lot of customers defaulted leaving me with uncollectible promissory notes. Before I knew it I had spent all my money including all the gold in the strongroom. I haven't recovered yet."

"How much is in the strongroom now?"

"Two stacks of junk bonds six feet tall."

"No, no, I don't mean that. How much gold do you have?"

"About 5,000 guilders."

"How many gold receipts are outstanding?"

"Not counting receipts covered by promissory notes, I estimate I owe 5,000,000 guilders."

For a moment nobody said anything. Then I said, "This is a desperate situation. You can pay off only one guilder for every 1,000 you owe."

O. K. said, "I feel like a savings and loan owner in the United States. I feel sick. I'm going to bed. See you at breakfast."

At breakfast we heard the rumors. Crossing the street, we heard the roar of the approaching mob, all wanting cash for their receipts. A run on the loan office was on the way! No time to lose. O. K. hurried into his office. We sprinted to our Time Machine and got out of there.

Now, we are back in the USA. This letter came from O. K. "Sorry we had no time for goodbyes. Everything OK here. Silent partners came through. The government is bailing me out with taxpayers' money. Big break for me. As richest man in Amsterdam, I pay my taxes with loopholes, not money."

The goldsmiths invented "bank credit" banking. They discovered they could loan a great deal of paper representing money with very little cash to back it up. These days I'm sure you have a checking account in a bank. You borrow $1,000. Your banker punches his computer and like magic $1,000 in "bank credit" is added to your checking account and a loan account set up showing you owe $1,000. You spend the borrowed credit by writing a check for $1,000 and when your check clears, the computer extinguishes $1,000 of "bank credit" from your checking account. Later you pay off your loan with interest. The computer extinguishes $1,000 of "bank credit" from your loan account making it zero. The interest is your banker's gross profit. Your banker does the same thing the goldsmiths did many years ago. He creates and extinguishes computer blips representing money and receives his interest in real money.

Creation of bank credit is called "fractional reserve banking" and creating money by a "flick of the pen." 80% of what we call "money in circulation" is bank credit.

Critics say that bankers should not be allowed to loan thin air as money. They say bankers should not be a privileged class more powerful than the Federal Government, that bankers should be required to loan real money the same as you loaning a friend a ten dollar bill.

Abraham Lincoln was a critic. He believed that the Treasury should provide all the money and credit needed by the U. S. economy. One way this could be done is the following.

Suppose that we, the American people, did not reelect any congressman or senator (except Henry Gonzalez who is a champion of UNITED STATES NOTES) and put in office a new group which would abolish Federal Reserve Notes. That would save the approximately 8% the Government is presently wasting borrowing Federal Reserve Notes. Next step: By law America's currency will all be UNITED STATES

NOTES which the banks will borrow from the U. S. Treasury at 1%. Good deal! Suddenly we taxpayers are 9% better off! What do you think?

Dear reader, you may doubt, or it may not have been made clear to you, that America--and other nations except Guernsey--are enslaved by bank-note currency aided and abetted by "bank credit." If so, the following may convince you. It was written by a man on the inside, a man who intimately knew the inner workings of money creation.

"Banking was conceived in iniquity and born in sin. Bankers own the earth. Take it away from them but leave them the power to create money and, with a flick of the pen, they will create enough money to buy it back again. Take this great power away from them and all great fortunes like mine will disappear and they ought to disappear for then this world would be a better and happier place to live in.

"But, if you want to continue to be the slaves of the bankers and pay the cost of your own slavery, then let bankers continue to create money and control credit." (Sir Josiah Stamp, President of the Bank of England.)

THE BANK OF ENGLAND IS BORN IN SIN

And away we go! Back to England in our Time Machine. I hate to tell this story because the dumb king is named William and the villain is named William also. I could change the names except that I am telling you the truth. The embellishments are fiction but the basic facts are true all through this book.

We land in London. This time we will be observers, we won't get into the action. The king is William III, the year is 1694. We are going to witness the creation of a money system that automatically enriches the investor class at the expense of the workers who actually produce the wealth of a nation. The Tallies were still in use. If William III had been wise he would have converted the Tallies money-system into a treasury-note system and the whole civilized world would owe him thanks forever. Instead he listened to the Devil in the person of William Paterson.

Birds of a feather flock together. William Paterson was a very rich man and he called a little flock together. They were all rich men. Said Paterson, "Fellows, I've worked out a scheme that will make us richer than we have ever dreamed. This king we've got now is like all heads of state, he wants a war if his own. He wants to kill off a whole bunch of Spaniards or Germans or Frenchmen or maybe it was somebody else. I didn't catch the name, he was mumbling when he told me. The king doesn't have the money to do a war so he wants us to loan it to him."

"Tell us more."

"Here's the deal. We tell the king that we will loan him a million pounds in gold and silver at 8% interest. That's a good deal for us but we insist that he does us a favor."

"And what's that?"

"He must allow us to establish the Bank of England. It will be a privately-owned bank owned by us but the name will fool the people into believing that it is a government institution. Our bank will be "by appointment of the king" and that will really convince the public that it's part of the government."

"Sound good but what does a bank do?"

"Banks provide money to the people by loaning it to them. Money is a responsibility of the king so England's money should be created by the King's Treasury. The king is a dummy. His Treasury is still creating Tallies but they are far too few to provide the currency England's economy needs. The king should order his Treasury to convert from Tallies to paper currency but he is failing to do his duty so we are going to do it for him. We are not only going to loan money we are going to create it for the cost of printing! We are going to make King Midas look small time!"

"The king is dumb, but will he go for this?"

"I'm sure of it. We'll get a printer to design some beautiful paper notes that are as counterfeit-proof as possible. We print on each note that it is redeemable in gold or silver. I figure that once we get started that 2% in gold is all we will need as a reserve. We will tell the king that we will print 1,000,000 pounds in bank notes. England needs more medium of exchange so we will tell him we are doing this for the good of the people. As we will manufacture our money for practically nothing we will always be able to loan it at a lower rate of interest than those who loan real gold and silver. In no time at all we will have a monopoly of England's currency."

"Sounds risky."

Paterson said, "I don't think so. As a matter of fact, I think the king thinks his government is supposed to borrow the money it needs. The lesson of the Tallies has failed to even dent his skull. I fully believe that once he has collected enough taxes to pay off the million pounds to us, he will begin borrowing our bank notes."

One of the gang spoke up, "I think I've got it! How much will it cost us to print, or should I say manufacture, a one pound note?"

Paterson said, "About one tenth of a penny."

"And what will a pound buy?"

"Oh, for instance, a pair of shoes."

"Think of that. We will be able to buy ten pairs of shoes for one penny. But better than that, we are going to charge interest on pounds that we create ten for a penny."

"You've got it."

"Next question. When the king starts borrowing our bank notes what does he give us for IOU's?"

"Government interest-bearing bonds. And here is where we are going to be smart. We will make so much money from the government paying us interest we are going to give some of it back to the king. We will tell him that after we have paid all our expenses we will return to him what is left over. Ahem, we will make sure that our expenses are managed properly."

Another pirate spoke up, "What a deal! The people will have to pay the interest with their taxes. The king collects the taxes and passes on the interest to us. We give enough money back to the king to keep him happy. Meantime, we are ripping off the people directly by loaning them pounds that we create ten for a penny. This is great! We are ripping off the people twice. Once directly and once indirectly."

Another money pirate said, "This is jolly good fun." And breaking out a bottle of scotch, "Gentlemen, a toast. God bless bank notes!" After the toast they had another drink and made up The Anthem of One World Bankers on the spot. They all started singing together, "God bless bank notes forever...," and after the opening line it was ad-libbing on their own.

Then Paterson went off to proposition the king. It took no persuading, the king was so eager to start his war that he was willing to agree to anything so long as he got his loan of a million pounds of gold and silver. After receiving the king's official okay Paterson returned to his gang. "We are now officially the Company of the Bank of England and I am the Governor," he announced to his gang of money pirates.

One of them spoke up, "The king is the king so he has a monopoly on England's money. He can do what we are going to do. We can't do it unless he gives up his monopoly and hands it over to us. Why should he? Why doesn't he tell his Treasurer to issue England's currency?"

"William III does not understand the lesson on money that the Tallies should teach him. He is one of those people who is hung up on the idea that money is gold, silver or borrowed bank notes. It is truly strange that some cannot grasp that money should be a servant. It should serve as a nation's medium of exchange. It should be neutral, it should be furnished by the government so that it is free of interest charges. The king should spend it or loan it into the economy. The point I am making is that ALL of England's money should be created by the king and absolutely nobody else."

"Paterson, you are a philosopher. Fortunately for us, also a rip-off artist. Tell us, what do you say that money is?"

"That one is easy. Money is anything whatsoever that a government with police powers demands in payment of taxes."

Paterson continued, "I will forecast the future for you. Nearly all governments will follow William III's example and do the same ignorant, stupid thing."

At this point we will allow one of the coconspirators to really see into the future, "Not Abraham Lincoln. Lincoln will have his Treasurer issue United States Notes."

"If he does, he will be asking for a lot of trouble and somebody will shoot him."

William III delivered England's economy to the money pirates, the Bank of England owners. He did much more than rip-off his own subjects. He set the pattern for other nations, like sheep, to follow.

When a nation hands over the creation of its currency to a cabal, operating under the name central bank, what happens? Many years ago, Thomas Jefferson told us:

"If the American People ever allow the banks to control the issuance of their currency, first by inflation and then by deflation, the banks and corporations that will grow up around them will deprive the people of all property until their children will wake up homeless on the continent their fathers occupied. The issuing power of money should be taken from the banks and restored to Congress and the people to whom it belongs. I sincerely believe the banking institutions having the issuing power of money are more dangerous to liberty than standing armies." (TRUTH IN MONEY BOOK.)

Our central bank, the Federal Reserve System, is limiting our liberty with the chains of government debt. Americans feel in their bones that our beloved nation is heading in the wrong direction. We don't trust Congress. We perceive Congress as a bumbling, inept body.

Congress can change that by giving us a sound economy based on unborrowed U.S. Treasury Note dollars. That would change the image of Congress from a bunch of people good only for raising money for themselves to a group of able statesmen.

Congress fails to perform its Constitutional duty to create our currency because it takes **BIG** money to get elected and reelected. Congress legislated away creation of the people's currency to the Big Bankers in 1913. The bankers give enough back to reelect supporters of the Federal Reserve System. You scratched my back, I'll scratch yours.

We need an election system that will negate the power of the money pirates.

The owners of the Federal Reserve Banks buy the legislation they want. If you doubt that, listen to the words of Meyer Amschel Rothschild, the banking genius who lived from 1743 to 1812, "Permit me to issue and control the money of a nation and I care not who makes the laws." Put a bit more crudely, Meyer Rothschild was telling us, "Permit me to issue and control the money of a nation and I can buy the politicians I need to enact the laws I want." The Federal Reserve System is America's Bank of England. It is controlled by America's money pirates.

GOVERNMENTS SHOULD SPEND ONLY
UNBORROWED MONEY

We carry some money and hand it to another when we buy something but most money is figures on paper or in a computer. Nature doesn't create money, man's bookkeepers create money. Governments mint or print currency. Non-intrinsic unborrowed **treasury** notes backed by balancing taxes is the logical paper currency. Key word is "treasury" as our government can spend treasury-note dollar bills directly out of its Treasury without borrowing. This avoids the trap of forced borrowing of more money to pay the interest on previous borrowings.

A government can estimate how much money it can spend by how much money its citizens are willing to repay. It is a truism that citizens can pay back the money their government spends on them but they can't pay it back plus interest. The interest isn't circulating in the economy, it is a mathematical add-on.

Money must be created first, tax collecting follows. The U. S. Constitution symbolicly errs in that Article 1, section 8, Clause 1 empowers Congress to collect taxes but it is not until Clause 5 that Congress is empowered to create money. This reflects the fact that the colonists were using foreign coins and private bank notes as America's currency and this misled them into putting the cart before the horse. They thought they could collect taxes first and spend the money later. Now we know government must first create money and spend it into the economy and afterwards collect it back into the Treasury.

If the colonists had really understood what money is and how it works they would have put money creation first, tax collecting second and would not have authorized Congress to borrow money. The big mistake written into the Constitution is empowering Congress to borrow money on the credit of the United States. When the Constitution was written, Thomas Jefferson was in Paris as our minister to France. When he returned he wanted to eliminate that clause by an amendment. Why don't we give ourselves and our children the gift of passing the Thomas Jefferson Amendment this year?

Debt is the way bankers make their living. A banker's merchandise is money but they shouldn't be permitted to create their own government currency. If they do, it is counterfeit merchandise. Bankers should be required to use genuine U. S. Treasury created money.

UNBORROWED money is money free of interest charges. It is the only kind of money Uncle Sam, the states and all other tax supported entities should spend. All U.S. Treasury created currency is unborrowed money. Please note with care the last sentence states "...Treasury created..." This reminder is given because the fact that the Treasury prints our currency makes it difficult for some people to fully grasp that our Treasury does **not** create Federal Reserve Notes. Treasury prints Federal Reserve Notes, it does not create them.

The word "issue" can be substituted for "create." Then we can say the U. S. Treasury prints Federal Reserve Notes and the 12 Federal Reserve Banks issue them by loaning them to the government and the public. Issuance of Federal Reserve Notes by exchanging them for IOU's makes Federal Reserve Notes a borrowed money system, commonly called a "debt-money system."

If Congress were to decide to use United States Notes as America's note currency, then we would say that the Treasury prints United States Notes and issues them by spending or loaning them into the economy. The Federal Government's issuance of United States Notes by spending them into the economy makes United States Notes an unborrowed money system.

Let us assume we free ourselves from the money pirates' bondage by using treasury-created currency. How does Uncle Sam help the states to enjoy the blessings of freedom from debt also? Henry Ford said, "It is so simple and easy some folks may not be able to see it." It is that easy. Uncle Sam can loan, as well as spend, treasury-created money without going into debt himself.

States, and all other tax-supported entities, should spend only unborrowed money thus **never paying any interest.** States are not permitted to create their own money, they are forced to use Federal Government money. The Federal Government should supply unborrowed money to states by means of loans at **zero** interest. Once a state is collecting the same amount of money it is spending it will be in equilibrium with an automatic balanced budget.

Because tax-supported government entities should pay no interest whatsoever, any interest citizens pay via their taxes is robbery by elected officials.

THE AMERICAN REVOLUTION: WON AND LOST

In CONGRESS, July 4, 1776.

The unanimous Declaration

of the thirteen united States of America.

When in the course of human events, it becomes necessary for one people to dissolve the political bands which have connected them with another, and to assume among the powers of the earth, the separate and equal station to which the Laws of Nature and of Nature's God entitle them, a decent respect to the opinions of mankind requires that they should declare the causes which impel them to the separation....

    July 4, 1776 the colonists declared their independence from England. 12 years before they were loyal to King George III. What happened in those 12 years to cause the colonists to go to war?

    Gertrude Coogan, in MONEY CREATORS, explains: "The fact is that the Bank of England manipulators, having gained control of British industry through frequent depressions, cast their greedy eyes on the commerce and industry of America, and set to work to lay hold of the money of the Colonists and, hence, the industry of the Colonists...

    "The money of the Colonial Governments was abolished by laws passed in violation of the American charters...

    "The Stamp Act of March 22, 1765, was not only taxation without representation, its terms **(forced the colonists to borrow at interest the bank notes of the Bank of England.)**...

"Benjamin Franklin, in his autobiography, stated that the refusal of George III to allow the colonies to continue to operate an honest colonial money system, which permitted freedom of the ordinary man from the clutches of manipulators, was probably the prime cause of the American Revolution...

"An honest, constitutional money system is the one thing that international money magicians will not stand for."

Today Congress has replaced England. Congress forces the American nation, in order to have a currency, to borrow at interest the money created by the Federal Reserve Banks. Congress, perhaps unwittingly, is the enemy of the American people instead of George III. It's a crime against humanity to force a nation's people into debt.

An example of colonial currency which George III abolished is the Bill of the Colony of New York which is shown in the chapter **FOUR LOGICAL MONEY SYSTEMS**. A second example is given below. For "create" or "issue" the colonists used "emit."

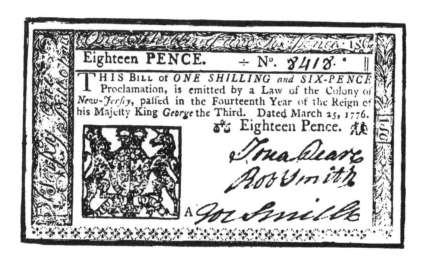

The above eighteen pence bill, it is a "bill of credit," emitted by the Colony of New Jersey promises nothing. Writing eleven years later, the majority of the authors of our Constitution refused to give Congress the power to "Emit Bills of Credit." This New Jersey bill, promising no redemption of any kind, surely must have contributed to that refusal.

So the money pirates of the Bank of England persuaded the English king to abolish the colonial currencies and in addition to impose the Stamp Act and other acts to extract from the colonists their gold and silver foreign coins. These actions set the trap, the colonists were going to be forced to borrow Bank of England bank notes. This would require IOU's from the colonists, the government bonds for bank notes trap!

So the money pirates of the Bank of England tried to force the colonists into the "government bonds for banks notes" trap but they didn't get away with it. The colonists weren't gullible like 20th century Americans, they were willing to give their lives to stay out of the money pirates' trap. Today's Americans are not only willing victims of the Federal Reserve Bankers' scam, our leaders praise the men who are victimizing us!

"Is life so dear, or peace so sweet, as to be purchased at the price of chains and slavery? I know not what course others may take; but as for me, give me liberty, or give me death!" cried Patrick Henry. The colonists went to war. Wars are expensive. Takes lots of money to wage them. Here is a sketch of the money, which in large part, paid for the winning of the American Revolution:

The sketch of the "Continental" is a composite.

The Continental Congress waged our Revolutionary War with currency they printed, but without power to tax. Money depreciates if after the issuing authority spends it into the economy it isn't balanced by being taxed back into the treasury. (Gold and silver <u>coins</u> excepted because of the worth of precious metal.)

Also, the Continental Congress lacked power to police the counterfeiting of Continental Currency. The English counterfeited a lot of it and later on the cry was heard, "Not worth a Continental." But, along with loans obtained by the colonists, the Continentals financed the winning of the American Revolution.

Spain stole tons of gold and silver from the Americas and opened a mint in Mexico City. Spain's Spanish Milled Dollar became the popular coin in the colonies and the Continental Congress accepted it as the unit of value for U. S. money instead of the English pound. Here are two examples of money issued by the states before the signing of the Constitution of the United States:

The pictured North Carolina currency promised redemption in Spanish Milled Dollars or the value thereof in gold or silver. This promise required that gold and silver be taxed from citizens and stored for future redemptions. Contrast this with the simplicity of the non-intrinsic system of the Colony of New York which required only protection from counterfeiting and equilibrium. One must admire North Carolina's motto, "A Lesson to arbitrary Kings and wicked Ministers," because this bill was printed in the middle of the War.

Here is a Rhode Island three dollar bill:

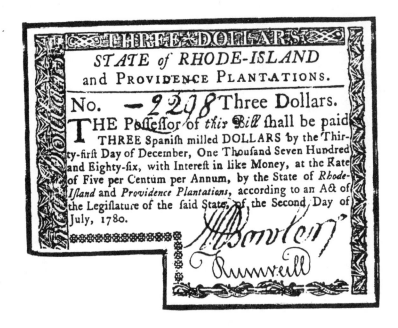

Contrast this Rhode Island currency with New York's. Rhode Island not only promised to redeem this bill with three Spanish Milled Dollars, it promised to pay interest at 5%. This is a terrible money system. It required the state to collect a greater amount of silver money than it paid out in paper currency! New York's currency was redeemable only by payments into the colony's treasury which is the way all currency should be. Rhode Island currency, redeemable for silver plus interest, must have been loved by speculators.

The treaty that ended the Revolutionary War was signed in Paris, September 3, 1781.

Now, a great tragedy began. The Americans won a war over the money pirates in 1781. Little by little the victory was lost. It took 132 years for the victory to be completely lost. In 1913, the Americans surrendered to the money pirates. Let us see how it happened.

Money pirates are helpless unless a nation can borrow money in which case they can bribe the leaders to accept the government bonds for bank notes trap. Let's look at the United States Constitution. Were the money pirates successful in 1781? Does the Constitution provide for Congress to borrow money?

Article 1, Section 8, Clause 2: **"The Congress shall have Power To borrow Money on the credit of the United States."** Those few words determined that the United States would be a plutocracy, government by the wealthy. Government borrowing forcibly transfers wealth via taxes from the working class to the investor class. (Taxes pay the interest investors receive on the government securities they own.) In contrast, a democracy treats all citizens as equals.

So the money pirates got government borrowing authorized in the Constitution which is their license to steal.

Because the Constitution authorizes the USA to issue money it has no need to borrow money. Thomas Jefferson knew this and he said:

"I wish it were possible to obtain a single amendment to our constitution. I would be willing to depend on that alone for the reduction of the administration of our government to the genuine principles of its Constitution; I mean an additional article taking from the federal government the power of borrowing money." (Skousen page 393.)

April 30, 1789, Washington sworn in as president.

Sept. 11, 1789, Alexander Hamilton appointed Secretary of the Treasury.

April 17, 1790, Benjamin Franklin died at the age of 84. In spite of the Constitution giving Congress power to borrow money, if the true nature of money were understood, no Congress would ever do so. Benjamin Franklin knew the Federal Government should issue and spend unborrowed Treasury notes. Bank notes are no good as a nation's currency because they automatically enslave the citizens with debt.

Although he had only eight months to live, had Washington appointed Franklin Secretary of the Treasury today's world would be a happier place with governments operating on unborrowed money.

Alexander Hamilton, who was the man Washington had appointed Secretary of the Treasury, took the United States down the road to eternal debt. The United States owed $75 million in war debt.

The debt had to be paid.

The United States, less than two years old, stood at the crossroads.

The Federal Government needed 75 million dollars. No problem, really. The Constitution gave it the power to create the needed money.

Hamilton, the Secretary of the Treasury, should have paid the debt with notes, which are money. Instead, Hamilton paid the debt with bonds, which are interest-bearing IOU's. A terrible decision! Thousands of Americans were holding war debt IOU's. Hamilton should have paid them with United States Notes. Instead, he plunged the USA into permanent debt via the sale of U. S. bonds for money. There are always bankers ready to issue bank notes. So you sell your interest-bearing bonds for bank notes that pay no interest. Then you pay off the old debt and have a bigger, growing debt. In fact, it has grown to today's $4 trillion debt requiring a yearly interest payment of $250 billion and going up! And our taxes will continue going up to pay it. A terrible waste of taxes! (Read Gertrude Coogan's detailed description of the events briefly described above. Begin page 196 of MONEY CREATORS.)

This is 1994 and our Treasury still issues IOU's named United States Bonds and T-bills, and sells them for bank notes named Federal Reserve Notes. And the American Bankers Association contributes tons of money to the campaigns of congressmen who vote in favor of continuing the scam.

Congress continues to borrow money to pay interest as if it were possible for borrowed money to catch up with interest!

During the War Hamilton led his men in a bayonet battle that helped turn the tide for the Americans. Hamilton was not fighting for Jeffersonian democracy, the democracy that Lincoln would later describe as government of the people, by the people and for the people. Instead, Hamilton admired the Bank of England, the English form of government and an aristocracy. He believed in government by men of wealth, a plutocracy. He was fighting to transplant England's Bank of England and form of government to the United States with himself and others of his class in charge.

As Secretary of the Treasury Hamilton was able to establish the Bank of England in America except he named it the Bank of the United States. He was able to get Congress to pass the legislation by bribing enough congressmen with inside information. He told them in advance that he was going to pay off the old war debt IOU's which had depreciated down to 15% of their value. The congressmen made a killing by buying at 15% and collecting at 100% plus interest. A great many patriots who had supported the war with their money were hurt financially. This did not worry Hamilton who believed that the common people should serve plutocrats. Hamilton took advantage of Congress' authority to borrow money and started the United States on the road to plutocracy.

Hamilton's bank, our first central bank, was allowed to die after its 20-year charter expired. Same for the second. We got our third, the Federal Reserve System, in 1913.

To Hamilton's credit, six years before he died from Burr's bullet, he wrote a letter dated August 22, 1798 to his successor at the Treasury.

> "My Dear Sir:
>
> "No one knows better than yourself how difficult is the collection of taxes even in modest amount if there be a defective circulation. According to all the phenomena which fell under my notice, this is the case in the interior parts of our country...
> "For these and other reasons which I have thought well of, I have come to the conclusion that our Treasury ought to raise up a circulation of its own. I mean by the issuing of Treasury notes...
> "This appears to me an expedient equally necessary to keep the circulation full...it will be easy to enlarge without hazard to credit.
>
> Alexander Hamilton." (Coogan, page 204.)

In that letter Hamilton told us the truth, Treasury notes, which are United States Notes, should be America's currency.

In addition, Hamilton pointed out the importance of the amount of money in circulation. Lots of money in circulation causes an upswing in the economy, a shortage a downswing. In 1929, Uncle Sam gave almost complete control of the volume of money to the Federal Reserve bankers. First, the bankers poured money into the economy which boomed, especially the stock market which soared wildly on borrowed money and credit. Then, the bankers yanked the money out of circulation and we got the Great Depression. Since then, starting in 1939, Uncle Sam spends enough money to give him part control of money in circulation. Regrettably, he spends the **wrong** kind.

Hamilton's advice to use the currency of democracy instead of the currency of plutocracy was ignored. It would be 64 years before any United States Notes would be issued. The man most people consider to be our greatest president issued them.

Birds fight for territory, so do animals, man and bankers. Hamilton's United States Bank, during its twenty years of life, aroused fierce competition from about ninety state chartered banks. Bank notes from ninety banks surely made chaotic currency for a nation but they kept us free from the chains of a central bank owned by money pirates. The state chartered banks issued bank notes until 1872 when the Federal Government taxed the state bank notes out of existence.

The War of 1812 was a strange war in many respects. England, again at war with France, began kidnaping American seaman from American ships on the high seas. We retaliated by attacking British shipping. The British answered that by landing troops and burning down all the Federal buildings they could find in Washington, D.C.

As always wars cost a lot of money and the Federal Government found itself in need. No problem, really. The U. S. Constitution empowers the Federal Government to issue money and collect taxes. Thomas Jefferson, who had another ten years to live, explains what to do on page 498 of Skousen's, "The Making of America:" (This is discussed in an earlier chapter but the clarity of Jefferson's words makes repeating them worth while.)

"... Jefferson therefore conceived of an ingenious device by which the American people could borrow from themselves without paying any interest. The following quotations from his writings will emphasize three points.

1. In a time of crisis issue whatever federal currency is necessary to save the nation.

2. At the same time impose a tax of comparable amount to redeem the extra currency within a designated time.

3. By this means the money goes out to buy the goods and services needed for the war

and then is siphoned back into the treasury through taxes after it has done its work, thereby avoiding any long-range inflation."

To provide sound money, Jefferson said, "Treasury notes of small as well as high denomination, bottomed on a tax which would redeem them in ten years, would place at our disposal the whole circulating medium of the United States; a fund of credit sufficient to carry us through any probable length of war..." Jefferson agreed with Hamilton, use federal currency, which is **UNITED STATES NOTES**, do not use bank-note currency.

The words of Jefferson given above describe the same perfect money system used by the Colony of New York. Long range inflation is eliminated by a logical money system as Jefferson pointed out. "Jefferson's money system" should be the money system used today by the USA. "Jefferson's amendment to the Constitution" barring Congress from borrowing money should be adopted. These two actions would give us economic democracy and lower taxes instead of the economic plutocracy with its overtaxation we have at present.

Did the politicians listen to Jefferson? Of course not, he gave them logic not campaign contributions. It would be 46 more years before Americans would have note money of their own.

So the debts of the War of 1812 had to be paid. No problem if Jefferson's advice had been followed but money pirates headed by Nicholas Biddle persuaded Congress in the usual way that what the United States needed was a central bank with the U. S. Treasury as its servant. Our second central bank was named "Bank of the United States" to fool the people. It was banker owned, just like today's Federal Reserve Banks.

Now comes the hero of New Orleans, Andrew Jackson. Peter Cook's Monetary Science publication tells the story:

"When Jackson ran (second term) for president in 1832, the issue was: No United States Bank... Jackson's argument was that this bank has the government's money and is protected by the Government; and yet the Bank defies the Government. **Who should really be the sovereign power...the bank or the Government?**

Jackson was elected by the common man who understood a grass roots President's language. He was given the mandate to abolish the Second Bank of the United States, and he was determined to abolish it. One of his supporters, Senator Benton made the following pertinent remarks, which clearly define the issue.

First; I object to the renewal of the Charter (1836) of the Bank as an institution too great and powerful to be tolerated in a government of free and equal laws.

Secondly; I object because its tendencies are dangerous and pernicious to the government and the people... it tends to aggravate the inequality of opportunities to make the rich richer and the poor poorer and multiply nabobs and paupers.

Thirdly; I object on account of exclusive privileges and of anti-republican monopoly which it gives to the (bank) stock holders. (This was later fully accomplished through the Federal Reserve Act of 1913.)

Jackson knew that Biddle (President of the U. S. Bank) could buy up enough congressmen to override any president's veto via the Hamiltonian corruption. Knowing this he removed the Federal funds from the U. S. Bank and refused to renew the Charter which was to expire in 1836. Federal funds were placed in state banks. In this way he broke the back of the Eastern money power...This stirred up a hornet's nest (The Money Trusts) who immediately started to create the 1837 panic with great success..."

President Jackson balanced the Federal Budget and had a surplus of $60 million. The surplus came from the sale of public lands.

President Jackson got down to brass tacks with Nicholas Biddle one day when he told him: (From LtCol Archibald Roberts' "Committee To Restore The Constitution," this quote is from Bulletin #357, dated November, 1991.)

"You are a den of vipers. I intend to rout you out and by the eternal God, I will rout you out.

"If the American people only understood the rank injustice of our money and banking system--there would be a revolution before morning."

It was good that Jackson killed Biddle's bank but he did not bring order to the issuance of America's currency . The United States Mint had been operating since seven years after the Constitution and then as now issuance of our coins was in accordance with the Constitution. That is to say the Treasury of the U. S. issued our coins. But coins are unsatisfactory as a nation's only money. Notes, paper money, were needed.

President Jackson said, "If Congress has the right under the Constitution to issue paper money, it was given them to be used by themselves, not to be delegated to individuals or corporations." Right on! Old Hickory, right on! Jackson's words are true in 1994. The 12 privately owned Federal Reserve Banks have no Constitutional right to issue our dollar bills.

Jackson did not get Congress to do its duty by issuing our note money. The void was filled by state banks.

It is evident that a modern economy runs on its money system. We pay for things with money. Nothing moves until money is exchanged. The foundation upon which an economy is built is its currency. Hopefully, our citizens will become interested in the birth of their currency, nothing is more important for their economic future. People have been brainwashed to believe money creation can only be understood by bankers. With this erroneous thinking, the money pirates have got us.

Even in 1994 most people have a vague idea that gold in Fort Knox or some other place is backing Federal Reserve Notes. In 1994, our paper currency is backed by a promise printed on each dollar bill. It is not backed by gold or silver. If our paper currency were backed by gold or silver our dollar bills would say so. The promise is **"THIS NOTE IS LEGAL TENDER FOR ALL DEBTS, PUBLIC AND PRIVATE."** Our Government is promising us citizens that our dollar bills are good for paying each other and for **paying our taxes.** You can think of our dollar bills as promissory notes if you wish. Their value is determined by what you can buy with them.

THIS NOTE IS LEGAL TENDER
FOR ALL DEBTS, PUBLIC AND PRIVATE

Now enters American history a GIANT. Pygmies hide his words and distort their meaning. The money pirates sneered at his currency and bought him enemies and ridicule.

Lincoln said, "The money power (Today the bankers who control the Federal Reserve System plus the American Bankers Association.) preys upon the nation in times of peace and conspires against it in times of adversity. It is more despotic than monarchy, more insolent than autocracy, more selfish than bureaucracy. It denounces as public enemies all who question its methods or throw light upon its crimes."

After reading what Lincoln said about them, it seems tame to call the international bankers of the Federal Reserve "the biggest robbers in history" and "money pirates."

A PRIMER ON MONEY

SUBCOMMITTEE ON DOMESTIC FINANCE

COMMITTEE ON BANKING AND CURRENCY

HOUSE OF REPRESENTATIVES

88th Congress, 2d Session

AUGUST 5, 1964

Printed for use of the Committee on Banking and Currency

———

U.S. GOVERNMENT PRINTING OFFICE

WASHINGTON : 1964

Page 48:

What would the Government have paid in interest costs if the "greenbacks" issued in Abraham Lincoln's administration had been issued as bonds?

Abraham Lincoln's administration issued a total of $450 million in "greenbacks," or "U.S. notes," as it was authorized to do by an act of February 25, 1862. If instead of issuing "greenbacks," the Lincoln administration had issued interest-bearing bonds, as urged, naturally, these bonds would still be a part of the Federal debt today. Assuming that the Government had paid an average 5-percent interest a year on this amount of bonds, it would have paid out $2.3 billion by 1964, or approximately five times the amount of money the Government would have borrowed. It is a fallacy to think, as many do, that the "greenbacks" were inflationary. In the only sense that matters, the relative or comparative sense, they were not. That is, $450 million in "greenbacks" is no more or less inflationary than $450 million in bank deposits or any other bank money created to pay for $450 million in interest-bearing bonds.

There are the official facts for all the world to see. Skipping the insanity of printing bonds and borrowing money, Honest Abe persuaded Congress to authorize issuance of $450 million in United States Notes, money much needed to finance the winning of the Civil War. This created no debt for the Government. It did create a debt for the citizens but it was free of interest charges. The interest saved, money citizens never had to pay, amounted to $2.3 billion by 1964. That amount is five times the amount of money Lincoln issued illustrating why we must conquer the bonds for bank notes scam by issuing our own treasury notes.

Lincoln's action favoring the people made the money pirates hopping mad. They persuaded Congress to repudiate Lincoln. They whipped Honest Abe and capped their victory by getting Congress to enact the National Banking Act of 1863.

After the Constitution was signed and before Lincoln, except for coins, Americans **never had their own money!** All note money had been issued by banks. Pictured is one of our first U. S. Treasury notes. Abraham Lincoln gave us our own United States Notes for the first time. He called them America's "greatest blessing."

Lincoln's treasury notes scared central bankers all over the world. Their "bank notes for bonds scam" was in jeopardy. If Lincoln's UNITED STATES NOTES continued as America's note currency, bankers would be demoted to loaning money only. Their privilege of creating money would be withdrawn and they would no longer be de facto rulers of nations.

The money pirates bribed Congress and put out propaganda United States Notes, the best money on earth--were no good. They sneered and called them "greenbacks." Even today, if you write your congressman and demand United States Notes for our currency, you will receive a reply written by a lackey of the Federal Reserve telling you they are no good.

The terrible price we pay because Congress takes orders from our Federal Reserve bankers is shocking. Let us suppose that Abraham Lincoln had printed bonds instead of currency:

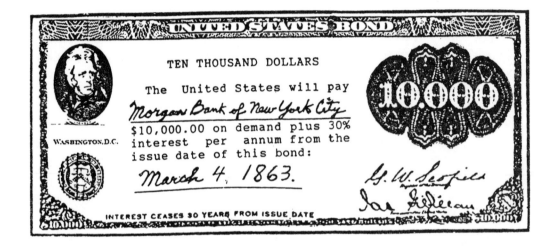

The reason this bond pays 30% interest is this quote from LINCOLN MONEY MARTYRED, by Dr. R. E. Search, page 44: "It is said that Lincoln and his Secretary of the Treasury went to the bankers of New York and applied for loans to the Government to carry on the war, the bankers replying, 'Well, war is a hazardous business, but we can let you have it at 24% to 36%...' Appleton Cyclopedia, 1861, page 296, says: 'The money kings wanted 24% to 36% for loans to our government to conduct the Civil War.'"

The bond above in our illustration is a $10,000.00 IOU paying 30% interest per annum for thirty years. Interest for one year would be $3.000.00. The interest paid every year for thirty years would amount to $90,000.00, nine times the amount of the bond. The $90,000.00 is interest so the principal of $10,000.00 would still be owed at the end of the thirty years.

Even if we change our interest rate to 8% instead of 30%, it's easy to see that Uncle Sam should quit printing bonds. It is also easy to see why Uncle Sam has a debt of $4 trillion which increases every day. The Grace Commission said that actually the Federal debt is $10 trillion. The debt, itself, wouldn't hurt us if it would just sit there and do nothing. It's the **interest charges** that wreck our economy.

Here is what the world's bankers really thought of Honest Abe Lincoln's greenbacks. By some kind of error it was published in a London newspaper shortly after the Civil War:

"If that mischievous financial policy, which had its origin in the North American Republic during the late war in that country, should become indurated down to a fixture, then that Government will furnish its own money without cost. It will pay off its debts and be without debt. It will have all the money necessary to carry on its commerce. It will become prosperous beyond precedent in the history of the civilized governments of the world. The brains and wealth of all countries will go to North America. That government must be destroyed or it will destroy every monarchy on the globe."

In other words, we should follow President Lincoln's advice. Lincoln, one of the wisest men who ever graced this earth, knew, as Franklin and Jefferson before him knew, money must be controlled by government. Here are his words:

"The circulation of a medium of exchange (UNITED STATES NOTES) issued and backed by the Government can be properly regulated and redundancy of issue avoided by withdrawing from circulation such amounts as may be necessary by taxation, redeposit and otherwise. Government has the power to regulate the currency and credit of the Nation.

"Government...should not borrow capital at interest. (Here Lincoln is agreeing with Jefferson and surely would have supported Jefferson's Constitutional amendment barring the Federal Government from borrowing money.)

"...The Government (The U. S. Treasury, not the Federal Reserve System.) should create, issue and circulate all the currency and credit needed to satisfy the spending power of the Government and the buying power of the consumer...Money will cease to be master and become the servant of humanity.

"... Democracy will rise superior to the money power."

Sadly, in 1862 Congress acted in the same way Congress acted in 1791 and acts today, congressmen and senators supported the plutocrats and sold the people down the river.

The money pirates persuaded Congress to eviscerate the United States Notes issued by Lincoln and then enact the National Banking Act of February 25, 1863 giving the United States a national currency controlled by private bankers instead of Uncle Sam. Bank notes issued by owners of state banks were replaced by private citizens who qualified themselves as owners of national banks by buying and depositing into the U. S. Treasury a million dollars in United States Bonds. The bonds paid interest of 6% per annum in gold. The deposit of the bonds gave the bankers authority to issue U. S. currency. The signature of the bank president was required. The bonds provided backing for the currency which was created for the cost, perhaps ½¢, of printing it. The bankers profited from loaning this ½¢ currency, plus the 6% in gold from their bonds on deposit, plus their control of the economy by increasing money volume with loans and then reducing it by calling in those loans for collection.

The National Banking Act was a giant step forward for the money pirates but it did not give them the centralized control with all the wealth and power they wanted. So they spent the next 50 years persuading Congress to install their "government bonds for bank notes" scam. The National Banking Act required the bankers to **buy** U. S. Bonds and deposit them in the U. S. Treasury. The Federal Reserve Act of 1913 turned this around and the U. S. Treasury began **giving** the bankers U. S. Bonds for their 2½¢ Federal Reserve Notes!

In 1872, Horace Greeley described the National Banking Act, "We have stricken the shackles from four million human beings and brought all laborers to a common level, not so much by elevation of the former slaves as by practically reducing the whole working population, white and black, to a condition of serfdom. While boasting of our noble deeds, we are careful to conceal the ugly fact that by our iniquitous money system we have nationalized a system of oppression which, although more refined, is not less cruel than the old system of chattel slavery." (Coogan, page 216.)

Serfs! You ain't seen nothin' yet. Wait until 1913 when Congress doubly attacked the American people with the Federal Income Tax Act and the Federal Reserve "hidden tax on the national currency" Act.

In 1862, James A. Garfield was elected to the U. S. House of Representatives where he served until 1880. He was Chairman of the House Committee on Appropriations and became an expert on money, credit and fiscal matters.

Garfield was elected president of the United States and took office in 1881. From his experience in Congress he knew what he was talking about when he said, "Whoever controls the volume of money in any country is absolute master of all industry and commerce." The money pirates, who at the time did not yet have 100% mastery of the USA, must have shook in their boots. Garfield was shot July 2, 1881 and died 80 days later.

To complete their control over the USA, the money pirates--America's biggest bankers with international connections--had to persuade Congress to establish America's third central bank. This required demonstrating the National Banking Act was not getting the job done and selling the idea that a central bank was the answer.

How the big bankers did this is told by Martin A. Larson in his "The Federal Reserve And Our Manipulated Dollar:"

"Since the National Banking Act had conferred upon the federally chartered associations of private banks the power to control the finances and credit of the nation they manipulated one devastating debacle after another, each calculated to confiscate the savings of farmers, tradesmen, individual manufacturers and thrifty workers who had pledged their property in return for bank-created credit. The worst of these catastrophes occurred in 1873, 1893 and 1907. Clever propagandists not only deflected the blame for these from the financiers, but used them to further their own interests by demanding a more elastic and centralized monetary system, one controlled by a great central private bank of issue, which would arrogate to itself far greater powers and profits than were possible under the National Banking Act of 1863."

The bankers got what they wanted. When Woodrow Wilson signed into law the Federal Reserve Act of 1913 the people who bought the 12 Federal Reserve Banks won the American Revolution. As Benjamin Franklin told us, the prime reason for which the colonists fought England was the right to create their own money. The American people lost that right to the Federal Reserve Banks in 1913. If we had won, our currency today would be United States Notes instead of Federal Reserve Notes. Not only did we lose control of our currency in 1913 but from then on our government has become more and more a plutocracy.

THE FEDERAL RESERVE AS OUR MONEY MANAGER

1913 was a year that reshaped the United States.

February 12, 1913 the 16th Amendment went into effect. This authorized our income tax laws. The law was acclaimed as a "soak the rich" law but was carefully crafted to protect the wealthy and powerful. (See Skousen.)

April 8, 1913 the 17th Amendment went into effect. This changed selection of U.S. senators. Prior to 1913, state legislatures appointed them, afterwards they were elected by a vote of the people. Some say this was a mistake and the United States is no longer a republic. For an excellent discussion read Skousen's, "The Making of America."

December 23, 1913 the Federal Reserve Act, the worst piece of legislation ever written, went into effect. Some say the Income Tax Act is worse. Both harm America. Both favor the wealthy at the expense of the workers who produce America's real wealth and both should be repealed.

In 1907, Senator Nelson W. Aldrich of Rhode Island had been a U. S. senator for 27 years becoming the influential head of the Senate Finance Committee. He had married into wealth and his daughter married into fabulous wealth. She married John D. Rockefeller, Jr. One of their sons, named Nelson Aldrich Rockefeller, became governor of New York.

In the fall of 1907, Senator Aldrich, trying to learn what currency is and how it works, was frowned upon by fate. In New York City, in the offices of Kuhn, Loeb & Company Aldrich met a young partner named Paul Warburg. It was a fateful meeting for the people of the USA. Three years later these two attended a secret meeting. The story of that secret meeting on Jekyll island in 1910 is well told by Eustace Mullins in "The Secrets of The Federal Reserve."

Paul Warburg was one of those Germans who immigrate to this country and speak in thick German accents. Sometimes hard to understand, he spoke plainly when he told Senator Aldrich and the others on Jekyll Island, "Fellow bankers, we got big trouble. More Americans think than I realized. To set them up for shearing, we've got to lie to them. We must convince them they need a central bank. Hamilton's central bank was allowed to die and the Americans said, 'Good riddance.' Nicholas Biddle's central bank was starved to death by President Andrew Jackson after he called Biddle a viper. Americans don't trust a central bank and they don't want to see another one established.

"So we've got to call our proposed central bank by another name. I propose that we call it 'The Federal Reserve System' and establish 12 branch banks all over the nation with none in Washington, D. C. The absence of a Federal Reserve Bank in the nation's capital will convince the people that the Federal Reserve System is not a central bank. Convinced of this the people will allow their legislators to enact into law what we want.

"Also, the name Federal Reserve System doesn't sound like a privately-owned central bank. Federal makes it sound like part of the Federal Government and by legal puffery we will disguise that we are the owners. 'Reserve' and 'System' are more words that will fool the people. We won't explain that reserve will be thin air and that system means the systematic removal of money from working people by our 'bonds for bank notes' scam which they will never believe even if it is explained to them. The interest on the government bonds will come to us and we'll spend as much of it as necessary to elect and reelect the politicians who vote for us. In this way we will use the people's own money to put them in our money trap.

"The so-called branches will insure legislative support. No senator or congressman will pass up the opportunity to have a Federal Reserve Bank built in his state. As you know we will run everything from New York through the Federal Reserve Bank there." (These are not Warburg's actual words but they describe the accomplishments of the conspirators.)

It took three more years and a heckuva lot of money for the plotters to foist the third central bank on the United States. Jefferson, Lincoln, Jackson! Oh, how we needed you in 1913. Who did America have in its hour of need? A strange man by the name of Woodrow Wilson who thought the world was a great big ivory tower. Wilson took orders from another odd duck, a political genius by the name of House. House wrote a novel telling how he was going to run the USA according to his ideas. House named his book, "Philip Dru, Administrator."

Quoted from Eustace Mullins, "One of the instructions outlined in Philip Dru is the Federal Reserve System. The Schiffs, the Warburgs, the Kahns, the Rockefellers and the Morgans put their faith in House and were personally represented at Jekyll Island..."

The Federal Reserve System had been in charge of America's money and credit for sixteen years when The Great Depression was caused by the Federal Reserve money system. First, a vast amount of money was loaned into circulation and then jerked out squeezing the money supply too low to sustain the economy.

In 1929, the Federal Reserve Banks, through the commercial banks, extended so much "bank credit" anybody and everybody was in the stock market buying stock on credit. (Dear Reader, please remember that "bank credit" is pen and ink money that exists temporarily until the banker collects it back at which time he extinguishes it.)

The bankers, frightened by the frenzy and fearful their loans couldn't be repaid, said to the borrowers, "Pay the money you owe us." A mad scramble took place as everybody sold stock at the same time to get the money to repay the bankers. The stock market plunged. Stock market accounts worth millions dropped to thousands, some accounts dropped to zero. Fortunes were lost and money disappeared from America's economy. As the bankers collected money they extinguished it taking still more money out of the economy. Collected money can be extinguished but bankers cannot "extinguish" uncollectible loans. Banks with too many bad loans went bankrupt. The solvent banks, afraid of going under, refused to make most loans and money in circulation dried up. The Great Depression was on.

Congress panicked and ran to the bankers who control the Federal Reserve System. As always, in the presence of their domineering senior partners, Congress was bewildered and said, "We don't want to upset you rich bankers as we want you to keep on giving us the money we need to get reelected but we've got a problem."

"What's the problem?"

"Our citizens are on street corners trying to make a living by selling apples to each other. That's okay. Some of our citizens are sleeping in the streets. That's okay, also. But some of them are beginning to catch on that the depression is caused by our partnership and that will never do. We might lose the next election."

"Don't worry. Soon, they will be in uniform fighting World War II."

"How do you know that?"

"World War II will be a continuation of World War I. We charged Germany with the entire cost of World War I. The interest alone is now so great there is no way Germany can pay. This will force Germany to elect a leader who will refuse to pay the international cartel of central bankers. Ergo, World War II."

"That will get America out of this depression?"

"Yes, war preparations will cause the Federal Government to pour money into circulation. When private enterprise doesn't put enough money into circulation to keep the economy healthy, the Federal Government must do so."

This made Congress happy. Polls show that wars are popular. Perhaps this is because of all the activity that takes place, jobs become plentiful, money flies about and so on. Maybe, we should create a large army for peaceful purposes such as reconstructing our slums, cleaning up toxic waste dumps and so on. Correction of our money system by installing the Thomas Jefferson money system would give us enough money to guarantee everyone, who wants to work, a job in such a reconstruction army. We human beings need to perform useful work, it gives us the feeling that we count. This suggested "Reconstruction Army," with jobs for all who can't find employment in the private sector, might even keep some members of gangs too busy to shoot people.

Then the Federal Reserve bankers frightened Congress by saying, "We are going to advertise that the Federal Reserve Banks will pay back the interest they receive on the bonds the government gives them."

Hearing this Congress collapsed in panic, "You mean you are going to stop paying us $500.00 for having breakfast with you and $5,000.00 for making speeches praising the Federal Reserve?"

"No. no. Don't worry. We are going to pay back only the interest we receive on the bonds held by our 12 Federal Reserve Banks. Of course, the pay back will be less our expenses and our expenses are substantial. We are not going to pay back the interest we receive on the bonds held in the commercial banks we own. On top of that, we make most of our billions from our control of the money and credit of the nation."

Congress said, "Why pay back anything? Wouldn't it be better for our partnership for you to pile up all the profit you can? We believe in capitalism, don't you?"

The bankers said, "Yes we believe in capitalism provided we are the capitalists, but this pay back gimmick is to blunt criticism we have received. We are naming our pay back, 'Interest on Federal Reserve Notes.' See how clever this is? We are admitting we create America's medium of exchange and that we are charging interest on it but we are claiming we pay the interest back to the Treasury."

Much relieved that their partnership was alive and well each member of Congress went back to his regular work of figuring out more taxes for the working man to pay while exempting all big donors to political campaigns.

The bankers and politicians began whipping up war fever for the coming war and enlisting movie stars to sell Government bonds. The more bonds the stars sold the deeper in debt Uncle Sam sank. An incredible amount of that debt is owed to the 12 Federal Reserve Banks and the commercial banks. Since the Fed Banks create money out of thin air and the commercial banks create about $9 out of thin air for each $1 they have, you can see that gullible Uncle Sam was giving away his bonds to the banks for nothing or 90% of nothing, a practice that is going on as you read this.

The 12 Fed Banks pay back to the Treasury their interest profit on government securities, the commercial banks don't. Any interest Uncle Sam pays is robbing the American people of that much money. That money should be spent on citizens' needs, not goofed off paying interest on debt. 60% of the taxes Uncle Sam extracts from you and me is goofed off on interest charges.

Readers wanting details of how the Federal Reserve conducts the biggest robbery in the history of the world should buy a copy of Margaret Thoren's, "Figuring Out The Fed."

Today, the Fed's official spokesman is the Chairman of the Federal Reserve. For the benefit of the big bankers with international connections, David Rockefeller sponsors the Trilateral Commission, Bilderbergers and The Council On Foreign Relations. Readers interested in the future plans of the international bankers will want to obtain information on these organizations available from several sources. Here is one: Liberty Library, 300 Independence Avenue, SE, Washington, D. C. 20003.

The money creators, the owners of the commercial banks and the 12 Federal Reserve Banks, control America with their ownership of America's currency. The big New York City international bankers who control the system, are thought to be--we are not sure as Congress prevents the Government Accounting Office from finding out--Lehman Brothers Bank, Kuhn, Loeb Bank, Goldman Sachs Bank and Rockefeller's Chase Manhattan Bank. These banks have foreign bank buddies so it could be said that the co-controllers of the United States are Rothschild Banks of London and Berlin, Lazard Brothers Bank of Paris, Israel Moses Seif Banks of Italy and Warburg Banks of Hamburg and Amsterdam.

Jefferson foresaw the Federal Reserve and called it a greater threat to liberty than enemy armies. How right he was! The Federal Reserve owners sink us ever deeper into debt. The deeper the debt, the more liberty is lost.

A dollar worth a dollar in 1913 has been milked down to about a penny today and as long as we leave the Federal Reserve bankers in charge even the penny will be worth less tomorrow and less than that the day after tomorrow! To paraphrase Aesop, putting bankers in charge of money creation is putting foxes in charge of chickens. It's okay to permit bankers to loan money but if you let them create money they will overwhelm with debt every nation on earth including the United States. To bankers, the principal of a loan is a means to an end--to keep the interest flowing to them. They "restructure" loans as necessary to keep the interest flowing. They can easily loan a hundred trillion dollars as long as governments permit them to create money out of thin air.

Talk about chutzpah! The chairman of the Federal Reserve and a committee of Congress hold hearings. Here's Congress talking to the appointee in charge of the "bonds for bank notes" scam so do they talk about correcting the system? No, they blame the people for America's money woes! They say Congress has been giving too many benefits to the people, the people are the problem. 37 million live below the poverty line but it is their own fault according to the Fed-Congress partnership. The people must tighten their belts, it helps if they don't put too much food in their bellies.

The real cause of the quarter trillion dollars in interest charges is never mentioned. The common people desperately need that $250 billion which is given to foreign and domestic plutocrats.

Money creation is the one function of government that should never be turned over to private enterprise. Congress did it anyway. Our central bank, the Fed, is a private enterprise the same as the central banks in England, France, Germany and all other countries where they are found.

As our money manager since 1913, the Fed has saddled us with a debt requiring an interest payment of a quarter trillion dollars yearly **and going up.** The Fed has flunked the course. Let's fire the Fed and get us a new manager.

Bill Clinton, elected president in 1992, is a member of David Rockefeller's Bilderberger group. It will be interesting to see if Clinton is a modern day President Jackson or just another buddy of the money pirates. If Clinton supports **SOVEREIGNTY** we will know he is on the side of the people.

SOVEREIGNTY: A GREAT IDEA WHOSE TIME HAS COME

No interest to pay loans for California, New York and all the other states! The states can quit printing bonds. THE SPOTLIGHT, 300 Independence Av., SE, Washington, D. C. 20003, published the following October 12, 1992. We are indebted to THE SPOTLIGHT for permission to quote from the article and wish to express our thanks.

The growing support for the **Sovereignty Resolution** was the topic discussed on the July 11 broadcast of SPOTLIGHT Editor Vince Ryan's weekly radio talk forum, Editor's Roundtable, when he interviewed Ken Bohnsack, author of the Sovereignty Resolution and driving force behind the nationwide push that has resulted in the endorsement of the resolution by not only 347 tax-supported bodies (city councils, school boards etc), but also by the U. S. Conference of Mayors, representing 1,050 cities with populations of 30,000 or more. Bohnsack can be reached in care of Sovereignty, PO Box 782, Freeport, IL 61032.

An edited transcript of the interview with Bohnsack follows. Questions by Ryan and his colleagues are after Q: Bohnsack's comments are after A:

Q: What is the Sovereignty Resolution?
A: The Sovereignty Resolution would make interest-free loans available to tax-supported bodies, such as state and local governments, including school boards. The tax-supported bodies can use these interest-free loans to build capital projects--not to provide day-to-day services. Capital projects are roads, sewer systems, bridges, public buildings etc. The tax-supported bodies can also use the interest-free loans to pay off existing debts.
Q: How many tax-supported bodies around the country have approved the

Sovereignty Resolution?

A: As of July 4, 347 tax bodies from around the nation have endorsed the resolution.

Q: Now the U. S. Conference of Mayors has endorsed the Sovereignty Resolution?

A: That's right, on June 24 the conference passed it on the floor of their national convention. As far as we're concerned this means an additional 1,030 cities have joined the call for initiation of the Sovereignty program. This represents about 80 million Americans across this country.

We are particularly indebted to the mayor of DeKalb, Illinois (Greg Sparrow), an economics professor who helped promote Sovereignty among his fellow mayors. His support meant a great deal to our efforts.

Q: What exactly is the text of the Sovereignty Resolution?

A: Here's the text of the resolution as approved by my home city of Freeport, Illinois. Obviously, each locality would substitute its own name when approving the resolution:

"Whereas the City Council of the City of Freeport must from time to time issue bonds to finance capital projects that are necessary to ensure the health and welfare of the citizens of Freeport, Illinois;

And whereas the city council recognizes that the cost of interest for bonds issued to finance capital projects is a great burden on the taxpayers;

Now therefore be it resolved by the city council that it does hereby express its support for the advisory resolution which requests that the United States Congress create money and instruct the United States Treasury to issue it as interest-free loans to the states and local tax-supported bodies for the purpose of capital projects and for paying off existing debts."

Q: There is a historical precedent for the Sovereignty Resolution and the kind of solution it proposes. Could you discuss that?

A: First of all, it's in the U. S. Constitution. Our Founding Fathers were brilliant enough to put it in there. You see, someone has to initiate an increase in the money supply. The Founding Fathers gave that power to Congress.

(The Continental) Congress used that power when they issued the so-called continentals which saved our country at the time of the American Revolution. The continentals got a bad name because the British government retaliated by counterfeiting them.

During the Civil War President Abraham Lincoln used the same power to keep our country together.

Q: The precedent for the Sovereignty program can be found overseas as well?

A: In the island state of Guernsey, located in the British Channel Islands, this same method was used that we are talking about. Guernsey took itself from a huge debt, unemployment and crumbling infrastructure in 1816 by issuing money, taxing it back in small taxes on butchers and imports.

Guernsey built capital projects, which is building wealth into your country. With that goes the production of steel, cement, heavy equipment and an increase in employment.

Guernsey has continued to do this and never has inflation. They have rid themselves of all their debts. Prior to this they had debts so great they were paying 80% of their total income just in interest alone.

That's what we are heading for in this country today. It is estimated that by the year 2000 interest on the federal debt will have reached a trillion dollars. There certainly is precedent for the Sovereignty Resolution.

Q: Essentially, Sovereignty proposes tax-supported bodies be given the opportunity to receive interest-free loans guaranteed by the American taxpayers. This, of course, is what the United States government currently provides foreign countries.

A: What is so exciting about these loans is, they will be used for the building of public projects. We are using the strategy in our proposal that the federal government would not use this method initially.

Our initial proposal is that these loans be issued to state and local governments.

However, if we are going to proceed this way, it is going to free up $900 billion currently in municipal bonds in this country in which state and local governments have their debts.

If the investors in such municipal bonds no longer have that vehicle, investors will still invest. Where will their money go? We feel these investments should go toward some of the strategic needs of our country. For example, changing saltwater into drinking water, alternative fuel research and development, certain environmental projects etc.

The wealthy people who are currently investing in municipal bonds should have a decent incentive to do that. I'm sure some of them will invest in money markets and certificates of deposit which are the source of building houses and business expansion.

Q: You quote Abraham Lincoln to the effect that: "The privilege of creating and issuing money is not only the supreme prerogative of government but is the government's greatest creative opportunity. By the adoption of these principles the taxpayers will be saved enormous sums of interest."

Abraham Lincoln: "The privilege of creating and issuing money is not only the supreme prerogative of government, but is the government's greatest creative opportunity."

Q: Is it not true, also, that not only will the taxpayers benefit from the enactment of the Sovereignty program but also that banks and the community as a whole will benefit?

A: Very much so. If we can fund public projects in the manner we propose-- through interest-free loans--then the $900 billion now funding them **(with the interest**

doubling and tripling the cost), these investment dollars can be made in the public sector. This would cause housing construction and business expansion to take off like crazy. By the admission of those bankers whom we've talked to and who understand our program, interest rates would then be less, and with the fact that so many more people would be employed, there would be more qualified borrowers to receive money in bank loans. The U. S. Conference of Mayors has said every $1 billion invested in infrastructure will create 50,000 jobs. We're talking about $300 billion invested. That's conceivably 15 million jobs being created.

Q: Would this involve construction of schools for local school districts, many of whom have endorsed the Sovereignty proposal?

A: Absolutely. Schools are currently going through the extraction of asbestos, and that's a major expense for local school systems. These are the kind of things that could also be financed with interest-free loans.

Q: School districts are suffering because many taxpayers have been voting down school bond issues.

A: That's right. School districts, as well as other tax supported bodies are often governed by state laws which says they can only borrow up to a certain amount based on their tax base. What is counted is not the amount of money borrowed, but the amount of money being paid back. So if you have a $20 million limit on borrowing, and you borrow $7 million, and your school district pays it back over a period of roughly 30 years, the district ends up paying back, actually, about $20 million. Thus, the district only gets a $7 million project out of a $20 million allowance.

With the Sovereignty program, we would now be able to get the real benefit of the amount of actual (dollars) borrowed and spent. Conversely, there could be money borrowed to pay off existing debts.

Q: What kind of response have you gotten from school districts that have the power to raise their own money?

A: When they finally understand what it is we are talking about, the light goes on in their heads, and they are happy with what we have proposed. In the beginning, however, there is a sense of concern and fear which we have to overcome. Sometimes the finance director of the school or the district is the most difficult roadblock in our way. After all, he or she has been hired at a hefty salary; and since they haven't come up with the idea, they are a little bit concerned that they might be shown up. That, of course, has never been our purpose at all. Most, however, are delighted with new ideas such as the Sovereignty proposal.

Q: Some major cities that have endorsed Sovereignty include: Harrisburg, Pennsylvania; Waterloo, Iowa; Lansing, Michigan; Sanford, New York; San Marcos, California; Fairmont, West Virginia: Port Arthur, Texas. These are cities all over the country. Likewise with other tax-supported bodies?

A: Thanks to The SPOTLIGHT, Editor's Roundtable, and Tom Valentine's Radio Free America, we have had people all over the country who have requested information on Sovereignty. They've used this information to approach their local tax supported bodies and present the program. These are good citizens at the grass roots who have done the job.

Q: The needs of the nation's cities have received a lot of attention in the wake of the riot in Los Angeles. Do you think this will give a new impetus, even a new legitimacy, to the Sovereignty program?

A: The word "legitimacy" is important here. We have come from nowhere, and now that the Conference of Mayors has endorsed the program, it will give us more legitimacy. Some of our nation's leaders understand Sovereignty enough that they have endorsed it. If the cities don't have to use so much of their resources to build a project, then they will have enough of their funds left over to take care of the social needs the cities provide.

Q: What approach have you taken in presenting your program to Congress?

A: Most recently I came to Washington in the company of Dr. Paul Davidson of the University of Tennessee, Dr. Robert A. Solo of Michigan State University and Dr. John H. Hotson of the University of Waterloo in Ontario, Canada, three veteran economics professors who support the Sovereignty concept. We held a forum on Capitol Hill to present the program and met with two members of Congress, Bill Orton (D-Utah) and John Cox (D-Ill.) and staff representing other members, Democrats and Republicans alike. We want a Sovereignty bill written and introduced in Congress. We want a bill with a number attached that we can promote around the country and urge people to write their own congressmen and senators in support of the legislation.."

OUR INTEREST CHARGES GROW EVERY DAY

'He Doesn't Leave Us Much Wiggle Room'

Reprinted with permission.

ST. LOUIS POST-DISPATCH

FRIDAY, APRIL 30, 1993

WHAT DO POLITICIANS MEAN BY BALANCED BUDGET?

It is impossible to balance a budget with borrowed money. The more borrowed the more out of balance. Uncle Sam collects all the taxes he can and then borrows money by selling U. S. Bonds and T-bills. When a politician says he is going to balance, or reduce, the budget does he mean he is going to spend all the money that comes in from taxes, declare the budget balanced, then spend borrowed money declaring "debt doesn't matter, we only owe ourselves?"

"Debt doesn't matter, we only owe ourselves," Franklin D. Roosevelt said that. It was untrue when he said it because government debt sabotages democracy by transferring wealth and power from citizens to the money pirates plus it guarantees inflation forevermore. It is untrue today for the same reasons plus foreign investors are buying our bonds. We now owe foreign investors in addition to American investors. Our politicians sell U. S. Bonds to foreigners to get the money to give away to foreigners via foreign aid!

And all those foreign banks! They aren't here for America's benefit, they are here for their own. Economically, the USA is the only nation that acts as if failing to protect its own citizens is a virtue and protecting them requires an apology. The USA is a family of 250 million people. Our family deserves a Federal Government that protects us from foreign armed forces, foreign economic warfare and foreign invasion via illegal immigration. If we don't protect what Americans have built, who will?

Because of the Great Depression, Roosevelt had an opportunity to take back creation of our currency from the Federal Reserve bankers. He did the opposite. He gave the Board of Governors of the Fed greater powers. That did not bring the country out of the Great Depression, it took World War II to do that. War poured money into our money starved economy. We have had an economy based on the god of war ever since. We need to change over to a god of peace that would employ the same number or more of our people.

A central bank and plutocracy go together. A central bank is the antithesis of democracy. In condemning the second Bank of the United States, Senator Benton pointed out a central bank creates currency that increases the gulf between the haves and the have-nots, makes the rich richer and the poor poorer, penalizes the worker in favor of the investor and increases both nabobs and paupers. Nabobs are the very rich.

In short, central bank notes are the currency of plutocracy not democracy.

The results of the Federal Reserve money system in 1992: Just 1% of Americans owned over one third of America's wealth, 99% owned less than two thirds. 37 million Americans have incomes below the poverty line.

A would-be democracy is stillborn if it hands over its money system to a central bank instead of its treasury department. The United States was lucky, we did not get a permanent central bank until 1913. We are in transition from mostly a democracy to mostly a plutocracy.

In 1991, the interest we paid on government debt consumed 60% of all personal income taxes. This waste was only 33% in 1985 so it doubled in six years and is headed up. Only 40% or less of our taxes will be spent on America's needs. 60% will go to the nabobs and others in the investor class.

Under our crazy Federal Reserve scam system, Uncle Sam would have to collect more than he spends to balance his budget. Even our money ignorant Congress understands that money must be kept in circulation but Congress, with no thought whatsoever of correcting the money system, slaps more taxes on us. Apparently, Congress thinks that Congress should keep money in circulation by spending our money for us. We don't need more taxes, we need to eliminate paying interest on government borrowed money. We need an interest-free money system based on the **credit** of the American people. We must free ourselves from the forced debt system of our central bank.

Because Federal Reserve Notes are borrowed money, Uncle Sam can never balance his budget until he abolishes them.

Anybody who understands a logical money system knows how to balance the federal budget. Exile our money pirates to the Bank of England. If the Bank of England refuses to take in their brothers, drop them in the Atlantic on the flight back. They will be at home among the sharks. Then use United States Notes as America's currency. After that 2 + 2 = 4, the treasury collecting the same amount of money it spends.

USA BANKRUPT?

We hear the USA is bankrupt. If the Federal Government is measured by the same rules as a private citizen it is so. But, Uncle Sam is not a private citizen. He can do something that not the UN, no foreign nation, no state, no county and no individual can do. Uncle Sam can create U. S. currency.

Unfortunately, Uncle Sam fails to personally perform his money creating duty and has delegated it to a group of favored citizens but this does not change the Constitution. He is still the only entity empowered to create U. S. money and he cannot run out because he can always create more. As he cannot run out of money he cannot be bankrupt.

It is true that Uncle Sam's money creating agents have made a mess of his finances. One of these days Uncle Sam may improve his balance sheet by devaluing our dollar bills.

The Federal Government tells us it lacks money for our own citizens' needs and they must do with less. If that is so, how come we are sending billions to Russia, Egypt and Israel and spending billions to support "one world" policing and CIA destabilizations?

At present, our government has no intention of paying off the national debt. It would cause us no harm if it would just sit and accumulate no interest. It's the interest on the national debt that is wrecking our economy by forcing us to pay all those unnecessary taxes that the Government then passes on to the nabobs who don't even need the money!

At present, is there a way to increase the national debt but not the interest on it? Yes. This can be done **because the Federal Reserve pays back to the U. S. Treasury the interest it earns on U. S. Bonds.** (See "Figuring Out The Fed," by Margaret Thoren.) Example: Uncle Sam gives the Fed a U. S. Bond for $100 billion with the agreement that the Fed will hold it forever and never sell it. In turn, the Fed authorizes the Treasury $100 billion in money. This will increase the national debt but not the interest on it because payment of interest to the Fed will be offset by the Fed's pay back to the Treasury. You are correct, that is a bunch of hocus-pocus, like the Federal Reserve System itself, but it gives our plutocratic "one-worlders" $100 billion more to further their ambitions to run the whole world from Washington, D.C.

INFLATION

I bought groceries today. I got a dollar bill for change. When I put it in my pocket it complained, "Hey, you, it's dark in here."

I took the dollar bill out of my pocket and we had a one sided conversation. I started our chat by asking a question, "I've been told you are in debt, are you?"

It said, "Yes, I'm a Federal Reserve Note. All of us are in debt. If you had the gumption of a goat you would know that I'm a piece of debt-money. I am an outstanding example of monetized debt. Now, let me tell you all about how this came to be. I was taken advantage of the moment I was born and blah, blah, blah...yackety yak...blah, blah, blah..."

My eyes glazed over. I wish I had more money, not talking dollar bills. To heck with how it's manufactured and manipulated. But I decided to humor the little creep. I said, "How much are you in debt?"

"It varies from year to year. This year it looks like it will be 5¢, APR."

I was afraid to ask what APR means but the smart aleck read my mind. It said, "That means that after a year I've got to pay an interest charge of 5¢ to the bondholder who loaned me to Uncle Sam."

I said, "How can you pay? You've got no change, you are a solid piece of paper."

"I pay with magic. I shrink. But my shrinkage is invisible until you go to the store and discover that where last year I bought a dollar's worth of groceries this year I buy only 95¢ worth. I call it shrinkage, you call it inflation."

IT'S MONEY IF THE GOVERNMENT SAYS IT IS

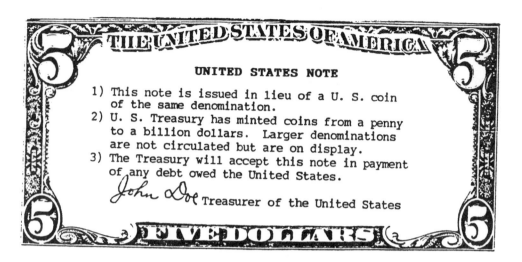

UNITED STATES NOTE

1) This note is issued in lieu of a U. S. coin of the same denomination.
2) U. S. Treasury has minted coins from a penny to a billion dollars. Larger denominations are not circulated but are on display.
3) The Treasury will accept this note in payment of any debt owed the United States.

John Doe Treasurer of the United States

Illustrated here are two currencies Uncle Sam could issue. The one above illustrates a note issued in lieu of USA coins. Coins belong to Uncle Sam so notes in lieu of coins would belong to Uncle Sam and **not** our central bank. Below is a bond that would be currency if Uncle Sam declared it so. This bond would belong to Uncle Sam just like all other U. S. Bonds except this one **pays no interest**. In both cases the illustrated currency spent by Uncle Sam into our economy would create no debt for him and no interest for us to pay.

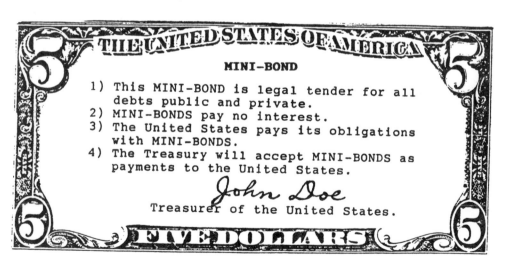

MINI-BOND

1) This MINI-BOND is legal tender for all debts public and private.
2) MINI-BONDS pay no interest.
3) The United States pays its obligations with MINI-BONDS.
4) The Treasury will accept MINI-BONDS as payments to the United States.

John Doe
Treasurer of the United States.

100% SAFE CHECKING ACCOUNTS

There is a better way for Uncle Sam to guarantee the safety of checking accounts than insurance. The savings and loan mess proved that. The insurance did not cover all the losses and taxpayers were charged billions.

Government insurance of accounts in S & L's insures that a crook can buy the business, loot it and get away with it because the insurance fund or the taxpayers will reimburse depositors for losses.

Let us separate checking accounts from savings accounts. We use checking accounts to pay our bills. It is devastating when the money in a checking account isn't there anymore because poor management has bankrupted the risk institution.

On the other hand, all citizens should be free to invest money as they wish. Money invested in a savings account or in other risk taking accounts is placed there in the hope of gain. These accounts should be caveat emptor, "Let the buyer beware." They can be insured by private enterprise but Uncle Sam should not be involved.

The better way to provide 100% safe <u>CHECKING ACCOUNTS</u> is to put our Treasury Department to work. Treasury should provide checking accounts for all citizens who want one. A fee should be charged for the service to cover the operating costs.

U.S. TREASURY HIDES U.S. NOTES FROM U.S. CITIZENS

Because Congress is the Federal Reserve's junior partner and the president is a member of David Rockefeller's planning group, it is not surprising the money departments in the U. S. Treasury act as arms of the owners of the Federal Reserve Banks. "Our" Treasury hides our money from us. The U. S. Treasury hides the American people's own money, **UNITED STATES NOTES**, in its issue vault.

A $100 U.S. note. There are 578,266 of them "in circulation"—including those (more than half, probably) held by collectors and 167,094 locked up in the "issue vault" at the Treasury Department. Yet the Act of May 31, 1878 mandates that $322,539,016 in U.S. notes be kept in circulation at all times.

This illustration is from an article in the populist newspaper, "The SPOTLIGHT," dated February 15, 1982 and reprinted in July, 1989. The above described perversion of the law is done at the behest of our money pirates. The money pirates, the plunderers of our economy, have brainwashed the public so successfully they are believed to be our defenders saving us from our elected officials. They have convinced the world that investors are better than workers, that plutocracies **are** democracies and central bankers are superior human beings deserving praise for stealing the people's currency.

FIGHTER FOR U. S. TREASURY NOTES

SPOTLIGHT February 15, 1993

Banking Critic Gonzalez Leads Fight to Reform Federal Reserve

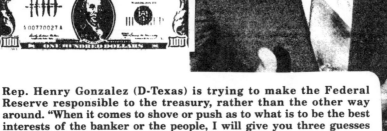

Rep. Henry Gonzalez (D-Texas) is trying to make the Federal Reserve responsible to the treasury, rather than the other way around. "When it comes to shove or push as to what is to be the best interests of the banker or the people, I will give you three guesses which you think will happen," he says.

Gonzalez said when he came to Congress, "three out of every five bills [in his pocket] would say U.S. treasury note." The populist congressman is looking to limit the power of the "almighty and powerful" Federal Reserve Bank.

Above, Rep. Henry Gonzalez points out that when he was first elected to Congress the Fed did not yet have a complete stranglehold on our currency. At that time three out of five of our dollar bills were U. S. Treasury notes and not bank notes of the Fed. In 1994, the Fed has us by the throat. All of our money is Federal Reserve Notes which automatically insert an interest charge in our tax bills. We no longer have three Treasury issued notes out of five in circulation. As you know, Treasury issued notes were interest-free to us citizens and would be this very day if Congress had the courage to issue them.

HENRY FORD AND THOMAS EDISON

Henry Ford, founder of the Ford Motor Company, and Thomas Edison, holder of over 1300 patents, were good friends. In 1921, eight years after passage of the Federal Reserve Act, Ford and Edison recognized that Congress was causing the U. S. Treasury to exchange interest-bearing bonds for non-interest-bearing Federal Reserve Notes.

In 1921, the international bankers were controlling the volume of money throughout the "civilized" world by means of the gold standard. President Garfield's statement is pertinent here, "Whoever controls the volume of money in any country is absolute master of all industry and commerce."

Also in 1921, Ford and Edison were interviewed by newspaper reporters. Substantial parts of those interviews are given below. (We are indebted to Peter Cook for permission to publish them from "Thomas Edison's Famous Interview On Money," a publication of Monetary Science Publishing, Box 86, Wickliffe, Ohio 44092-0086. $3.50 plus $2.00 P & H. Send for catalog.)

In the interviews Ford calls UNITED STATES NOTES, "redeemable non-interest bearing currency" and Edison calls them, "United States bills."

In 1921, Uncle Sam needed $30 million to complete the big Muscle Shoals dam. Taxes were insufficient and Uncle Sam proposed to issue 30-year bonds paying 4 per cent.

Ford was interviewed by a reporter. We begin our quote near the middle:

Ford said, "At the end of 30 years the Government not only has to pay back the $30,000,000 but it has to pay 120 per cent interest, literally has to pay $66,000,000 for the use of $30,000,000 for 30 years. And all the time it is the Government's own

---

money. The money sellers never created it; they got it from the Government originally. The Government first gave credit, and then must pay for the use of what it gave.

"Think of it, could anything be more childish, more unbusinesslike? Now I see a way by which our Government can get this great work completed without paying a nickel to the money sellers. It's as sound as granite and there's just one thing hard about it; it's so simple and easy that, maybe, some folks can't see it.

"The Government needs $30,000,000. That's 1,500,000 $20 bills. Let the Government issue those bills and with them pay every expense connected with the completion of the dam. The dam completed, we can set the whole works running, and within a shorter time than you would suppose, the entire $30,000,000 currency issued can be retired out of the earnings of the plant."

"But," I asked, "suppose the contractor would be unwilling to accept that kind of currency in payment?"

"There's not that kind of suppose in the situation at all," said Mr. Ford smiling. "He would take Government bonds in payment, wouldn't he? Certainly.

"Here," said the manufacturer, pulling a $20 bill from his pocket, "he wouldn't hesitate about taking that kind of money, would he? Of course not. Well, what is there behind a bond, or this bill, that make them acceptable? Simply the good faith and credit of the American people. And $20 bills issued by the Government to complete this great public improvement would have just as much of the good faith and credit of the American people behind them as any bond or other American currency ever issued. You see, it's just a question of faith in the American people."

"But your plan would upset the money system of the world and might work incalculable harm."

"Not necessarily: not at all. We need not abolish anything. We need not even abolish the gold standard. Simply forget there is any such thing as a gold standard and whenever the Government needs money for a great, serviceable and profitable public improvement, instead of thinking of bonds and their drag of interest charges, think of redeemable non-interest bearing currency.

"Do you realize how the interest charges of our Government mount up? Do you appreciate that 80 cents of every dollar raised by taxation is spent on payment of interest? The national debt is nothing more nor less than the nation's interest liability pile. Every public improvement this country makes means an increase in the national debt. Here's a way to get the improvements without increasing the debt. The interest load is breaking down our whole financial system; we've got to stop somewhere."

"But, in a sense, there would be no security behind this kind of money," it was suggested.

"There would be the best security in the world. Here you have a river capable of furnishing 1,000,000 horse power. It has been here for say, 100,000,000 years. It will be here as long as there is rain and mountains to send the rain into the rivers. This energy is wealth in a most productive form. Now which is the more imperishable, the more secure, this power site and its development, or the few barrels of gold necessary to make $30,000,000? This site, with its power possibilities, will be here long after the Treasury building is an ancient ruin."

"But have you worked out a standard of values?" Mr. Ford was asked.

"Yes, we have... It's simply a case of thinking and calculating in terms different from those laid down to us by the international banking group, to which we have grown so accustomed that we think there is no other desirable standard. We should change our minds on that question. The only difference between this currency plan and the bond plan is that there's no interest to be paid and the money merchants, who do nothing to build the dam and deserve nothing, will get nothing."

"But how is all this going to stop war?"

"Simply because if tried here at Muscle Shoals, this plan will prove to be so overwhelmingly and amazingly successful that the American people will never again consent to issuance of an interest-bearing bond for an internal improvement. When the Government needs money it will raise it by issuing currency against its imperishable natural wealth. Other countries, seeing our success, will do likewise. The function of the money seller will have disappeared."

"What would be the attitude of other countries about accepting this money based on Muscle Shoals?"

"There need be no difficulty about that. Some of our currency even today is not acceptable to foreign countries in payment of debts. Gold is the international basis. Muscle Shoals is a national, not an international matter. The money would only be for use at home."

"Do you expect Congress will act favorably on your suggestion?"

"I don't know as to that. Maybe they won't. But I'll bet the average American citizen will see the righteousness, the soundness and the common sense, of this thing.

"No matter what becomes of this suggestion, I shall...do my utmost to save the people from the enormous interest charges."

Thomas Edison's interview was published in the New York Times, December 6, 1921. Omitting the first third:

Edison: "Gold and money are separate things, you see. Gold is the trick mechanism by which you can control money.

"Gold is not money until the people of the United States and other nations put their stamp on it. It is not the gold that makes the dollar. It is the dollar that makes the gold. Take the dollar out of the gold, and leave it merely yellow metal, and it sinks in value. Gold is established by law, just as silver was. When silver was demonetized the former so-called dollar became worth about 50 cents."

"But would not Mr. Ford's suggestion that Muscle Shoals be financed by a currency issue raise some objections?" Mr. Edison was asked.

"Certainly. There is a complete set of **misleading slogans kept on hand for just such outbreaks of common sense** among the people. The people are so ignorant of what they think are the intricacies of the money system that they are easily impressed by big words. There would be new shrieks of 'fiat money' and 'paper money' and 'greenbackism' and all the rest of it--the same old cries with which the people have been shouted down from the beginning.

"...I think we are getting a sound idea on the money question. The people have an instinct which tells them something is wrong, and that the wrong somehow centers in money. They have an instinct, also, when a proposal is made in their interest or against them.

"Now, as to paper money, so called, every one knows that paper money is the money of civilized people. The higher you go in civilization the less actual money you see. It is all bills and checks. What are bills and checks? Mere promises and orders. What are they based on? Principally on two sources--human energy and the productive earth. Humanity and the soil--these are the only real bases for money.

"...There is just one rule for money. Too little or too much are both bad..."

"Then you see no difference between currency and Government bonds?" Mr. Edison was asked.

"...there is a difference...(and) if people ever get to thinking of bonds and bills at the same time, the game is up.

"Now, here is Ford proposing to finance Muscle Shoals by an issue of currency. Very well, let us suppose for a moment that Congress follows his proposal. Personally, I don't think Congress has enough imagination to do it, but let us suppose it does. The required sum is authorized--say $30,000,000. <u>The bills are issued directly by the Government, as all money ought to be.</u> When the workmen are paid off they receive these United States bills. When the material is bought it is paid in these United States bills. Except that perhaps the bills may have an engraving of a water dam, instead of a railroad train and a ship, as some of the Federal Reserve notes have, they will be the same as any other currency put out by the Government, that is, they will be money. They will be based on the public wealth already in Muscle Shoals, and their circulation will increase the public wealth, not only the public money but the public wealth--real wealth.

"When these bills have answered the purpose of building and completing Muscle Shoals, they will be retired by the earnings of the power dam. That is, the people of the United States will have all they put into Muscle Shoals and all they can take out for centuries --the endless wealth-making water power of that great Tennessee River-- with no tax and no increase in the national debt."

"But suppose Congress does not see this, what then?"

"Then Congress must fall back on the old way of doing business. It must authorize an issue of bonds. That is, it must go to the money brokers and borrow enough of our own national currency to complete great national resources, and we must pay interest to the money brokers for the use of our own money.

"That is to say, under the old way any time we wish to add to the national wealth we are compelled to add to the national debt.

"Now, that is what Henry Ford wants to prevent. He thinks it is stupid and so do I, that for a loan of $30,000,000 of their own money the people of the United States should be compelled to pay $66,000,000--that is what it amounts to with interest. People who will not turn a shovelful of dirt nor contribute a pound of material will collect more money from the United States than will the people who supply the material and do the work. That is the terrible thing about interest. In all our great bond issues the interest is always greater than the principal. All of the great public works cost more than twice the actual cost, on that account. Under the present system of doing business we simply add 120 to 150 per cent of the stated cost.

"But here is the point; If our nation can issue a dollar bond it can issue a dollar bill. The element that makes the bond good makes the bill good, also. The difference between the bond and the bill is that the bond lets the money brokers collect twice the amount of the bond and an additional 20 per cent, whereas the currency pays nobody but those who contribute to Muscle Shoals in some useful way.

"If the Government issues bonds, it simply induces the money brokers to draw $30,000,000 out of the other channels of trade and turn it into Muscle Shoals; if the Government issues currency, it provides itself with enough money to increase the national wealth at Muscle Shoals without disturbing the business of the rest of the country. And in doing this it increases its income without adding a penny to its debt.

"It is absurd to say that our country can issue $30,000,000 in bonds and not $30,000,000 in currency. Both are promises to pay, but one promise fattens the usurer, and the other helps the people. If the currency issued by the Government were no good, then the bonds issued would be no good either. It is a terrible situation when the Government to increase the national wealth, must go into debt and submit to ruinous interest charges at the hands of men who control the fictitious values of gold.

"Look at it another way. If the Government issues bonds, the brokers will sell them. The bonds will be negotiable; they will be considered as gilt-edged paper. Why? Because the Government is behind them, but who is behind the Government? The people. Therefore it is the people who constitute the basis of Government credit. Why then cannot the people have benefit of their own gilt-edged credit by receiving non-interest bearing currency on Muscle Shoals, instead of the bankers receiving the benefit of the people's credit in interest bearing bonds?

"The people must pay anyway; why should they be compelled to pay twice, as the bond system compels them to pay? The people of the United States always accept their Government's currency. If the United States Government will adopt this policy of increasing its national wealth without contributing to the interest collector--for the whole national debt is made up of interest charges--then you will see an era of progress and prosperity in this country such as could never have come otherwise."

OUR IGNORANCE OF MONEY MAY BE EXCUSABLE

"Benjamin Franklin, advocate of scientific and honest money, was born in 1706...His letters written on matters of public business from 1757 to 1790 are most revealing as to the true motives that actuated the British in their economic war upon America. Strangely, they are omitted in current biographies. No doubt the reason for this is that Franklin discusses honest money too frequently for the comfort of our present day money creators. Were it not for his writings there would be little reference available to the public concerning the basic cause of the American War for Independence." (Coogan, page 178.)

June 13, 1767, Franklin described a meeting of the British parliament. The subject was how to wring the most money out of the American Colonies: "Grenville said, '...make paper money for the Colonies, issue it upon loan there, take the interest...'" Sound familiar? It's the same scam the Federal Reserve Bankers are working against America in 1994!

No doubt the plutocrats in charge of our Government hope you will continue to believe that a tax on tea was the prime cause of the American War for Independence.

James P. Fitzgerald in THE NATIONAL EDUCATOR, October 1993: "Everyone recognizes the unique part played by money in the economy. A Rothschild banker said, 'Let me create and control the money of a nation and I care not who makes the laws.'

"In spite of this almost universal recognition of the importance of money, the politicians and press have been persuaded to conceal the fact that government has handed over to the banks its sovereign right to create and control the nation's money. Thus, the Rothschild desire has been fulfilled; government makes the laws but the banks create and control the nation's money supply. This odd arrangement took effect in December, 1913 under passage of the Federal Reserve Act."

Failure of the press to publicize theft of America's money system is easily explained. Federal Reserve Bank owners and their wealthy beneficiaries bought America's major media. It follows the press is not only silent regarding the theft, it praises it! Here is an example:

Headline October 20, 1993 in Los Angeles Times: "Too Important to Politick With." The editorial then tells us Henry Gonzalez is trying to reform the Federal

---

Reserve and is proposing to politicize the Fed which should be insulated from such pressures. Thomas Edison said that misleading slogans are kept on hand in case of an outbreak of common sense. Gonzalez's proposals are common sense so the Times reworded one of the money pirates' favorite slogans, "Don't politicize the Fed!" Political, politick and politicize are scare words that are supposed to keep you from thinking. If you calmly consider what the Times is saying, it is this--you should have no control, through your elected representatives, over your money system. You should be a sheep and continue to permit operation of America's money system by a bureacracy of unelected people.

    DO POLITICIZE THE FEDERAL RESERVE! No question about it, we should politicize the Fed. For over 200 years Congress has operated the U. S. Mint at a profit.* Congress has managed well, the Fed the opposite. For 80 years the Fed has owned and been in charge of our paper money with the result the USA has a loss of $4 to $10 trillion dollars. The loss is taxpayers' loss, not the bankers. Oh, no, no. They are a bunch of fat cats while the people are paying more taxes every day and wondering how to pay for medical care.

    Until one is exposed to the truth, ignorance of what money really is and how it is created may be excusable. Change of our money system is possible but more probable is when the interest on the national debt gobbles up money faster than the government can borrow it the plutocrats will start over by borrowing new bank notes to replace our present ones at a ratio of one to a thousand or some such figure.

    Change may be possible but listen to the words of Niccolo Machiavelli, 1469-1527, Italian author and statesman famous for his book, "THE PRINCE:"

> *"There is no more delicate matter to take in hand, nor more dangerous to conduct, nor more doubtful of success, than to step up as a leader in the introduction of changes. For he who innovates will have for his enemies all those who are well off under the existing order of things, and only lukewarm supporters in those who might be better off under the new."*

    * Page 53, "THE 200 YEAR DEBATE, Who Shall Issue The Nation's Money," by former Washington State senator, Jack Metcalf. Other sources for truth in money are referenced all through the body of this work.

HOPE

If all the states elect a Henry Gonzalez we can change our debt money system to the system advocated by Thomas Jefferson and Abraham Lincoln.

Let us suppose it happens. Then a possible reform program could be:

1) Abolish Federal Reserve Notes, replace with UNITED STATES NOTES.

2) Bar Congress from borrowing money. Amend the Constitution to that effect.

3) Install Ken Bohnsack's "Sovereignty" to finance all tax supported bodies below the Federal Government.

4) Abolish the Federal Reserve System. Assign all its functions to the U. S. Treasury. Change the 12 Federal Reserve Banks to arms of the Treasury.

5) Recover or redeem all outstanding U. S. Bonds and never again print an IOU. (See 2) above.)

6) Bar banks from creating "bank credit" i. e. no more fractional reserve banking.

7) U. S. Treasury will provide ONLY special, strictly regulated U. S. banks with the money required to finance the economy of the United States. The Treasury will loan them the money at 1% interest.

8) The Constitution empowers Congress, not the president, to provide the medium of exchange for the United States. To satisfy this Constitutional requirement Congress, not the president, will appoint the Treasurer of the United States.

9) Congress will direct the Treasurer to keep outgo balanced by income. Some years it may be necessary to increase or decrease the money supply in which case Congress will order the Treasurer to do so.

This plan proposes that Congress create all our money. This turns off some people who say they don't trust Congress. For over 200 years Congress has done a good job creating our coin money. The good job Congress has done with our coins demonstrates that our elected representatives can be trusted to create all of our money.

Congress did a good job when it cooperated with President Lincoln in issuing

---

note money during the Civil War. As the record shows, that action of Congress saved the people of the United States many billions of dollars.

Congress did a good job issuing Silver Certificates. Silver certificates were not notes of the Federal Reserve System, they were dollar bills that belonged to us, the American people. When issued by Uncle Sam we never had to pay interest on them with our taxes. Here is a 1953 Silver Certificate:

Here is a United States Note issued in 1963 proving that we had at least some debt-free, interest-free dollar bills as late as 1963. Although two dollar bills have never been popular, Congress deserves credit for every United States Note ever issued. The Federal Reserve bankers continually tighten the noose around our necks and today we see nothing but borrowed Federal Reserve Notes in circulation.

No question about it, Congress should exercise its Constitutional empowerment and create all our money in the United States Treasury.

CONGRESSMAN JOE

Once upon a time there was a congressman named Joe. In a dream he was visited by the Spirit of Two Forefathers. The Spirit said, "I'm leaving you a priceless gift. You will see it when you awaken."

When Joe awoke he was amazed to find a goose in his bed. Thankful the goose hadn't relieved himself, or herself, Joe grabbed the goose and threw it out the door. Just in time! The goose squatted a bit and let go. Let go a golden egg! Joe charged out the door, pocketed the egg, kissed the goose, built it a pen, bought it the biggest bag of goose feed in town and went to see a gold assayer. "This egg is pure gold," said the assayer.

In all the excitement, Joe had not seen the envelope left on his dresser by the Spirit of his Forefathers. An ill wind arose and blew the envelope off the dresser and it lodged behind it.

On the way home from the assayer, Joe met a man with shifty eyes who was walking with a rooster. "Biggest rooster I ever saw," said Joe.

"He's got to be big. He lays thirty pieces of silver at a time."

Congressman Joe said, "I've never understood farm problems but I thought hens laid eggs."

Shifty said, "I didn't say this rooster lays eggs, I said he lays thirty pieces of silver all at one time, plink, plink, plink."

"You aren't going to believe this, but I've got a goose that lays golden eggs. She just came to work this morning."

"Real gold?"

"Pure solid gold. Feel how heavy this one is. No wonder it goes klunk when she lays it."

Shifty inspected the egg and said, "You are in serious trouble. President Roosevelt just this morning signed the bill making it illegal for Americans to own gold."

In disbelief, "Even congressmen?"

"Especially congressmen. But I can save you provided you follow my instructions to the letter."

"How?"

"It so happens that I wrote the bill. I am a central banker and we central bankers always get special privileges from gullible governments. It is okay for me to own gold. I will do you the great favor of taking from you the goose that lays the golden eggs. In return, I'll slip these thirty pieces of silver into your pocket while nobody is watching. And, on top of that, I'll give you my giant rooster."

So the deal was done. Every morning after that the banker got a golden egg. Joe is still waiting for the rooster to come through with more silver.

The banker built an enormous mansion on top of a big hill. Joe goes up there every two years, hat in hand, and pleads for contributions. Shifty gives him thirty pieces of silver from time to time as a reminder of who owns who. (For definition of thirty pieces of silver see Matthew 26:15, 27:3-10.)

The other day Joe found the envelope that was hidden behind his dresser. Inside was a letter:

Dear Joe,

The goose that lays golden eggs is a symbol of The Power To Create Money. Never give her away. Never give away the power to create money given you by The Constitution.

A government's greatest power is its ability to spend unborrowed money. Never make the mistake of printing government bonds and using them as IOU's to borrow bank notes. Never spend so much as one penny of borrowed money. Spend only our own unborrowed money created by our own United States Treasury.

Sincerely Yours,

Th Jefferson
A. Lincoln

The END of The Money Pirates.

REFERENCES

Books and booklets referenced in THE MONEY PIRATES are available from many sources. Here are three excellent ones:

Liberty Library, 300 Independence Avenue, S. E., Washington, D. C. 20003.

Monetary Science Publishing, Wickliffe, Ohio 44092-0086.

OMNI Publications, PO Box 900566, Palmdale, CA 93590.

INDEX